BY THE SAME AUTHOR

- ☆ My Unconsidered Judgement
- ☆ What Manner of Man
- ☆ Lost Continent
- ☆ Fallen Sun
- ☆ Briton Hadden, Co-Founder of *Time*
- ☆ Adlai Stevenson of Illinois
- ☆ Thailand, an Introduction to Modern Siam
- ☆ Two Minutes to Noon
- ☆ TR, the Story of Theodore Roosevelt and His Influence on Our Time
- ☆ The Emperor's Sword: Japan v. Russia in the Battle of Tsushima
- ☆ A Concise History of Japan

George Washington at Princeton. Oil on canvas painted by Charles Willson Peale in 1779.

WINTER QUARTERS

*George Washington and the Continental Army
at Valley Forge*

Noel F. Busch

Liveright · New York

ISBN: 0-87140-587-3
Library of Congress Catalog Card Number: 73-89217
1.987654321

Designed by Dennis J. Grastorf
Manufactured in the United States of America

ILLUSTRATIONS

PREFACE

WHILE INVESTIGATING SOME much more recent happenings in Washington not long ago, I chanced to learn of an incident that had occurred in the nearby, and then much bigger, town of Alexandria, Virginia, on October 16, 1824. This was the day on which the Marquis de Lafayette was scheduled to appear there in the course of his farewell visit to the United States. In honor of his arrival, a splendid arch of evergreen boughs had been constructed on the street along which his carriage was to pass. Perched on top of this arch was a large live eagle whose role in the proceedings was to screech and flap his eight-foot wings just as the renowned visitor approached.

The problem that naturally arose here was how to persuade the eagle to perform on cue. To this end, a smallish boy was concealed in the foliage in such a way that, by yanking on a string attached to one of the eagle's claws, he could presumably elicit the desired response. According to contemporary accounts the device worked perfectly. However, what gave the story its special fascination for me was that its narrator, Mrs. Hallie Ramsay Conger, had gotten it firsthand from the prompter concealed in the foliage. He was her grandfather, George Washington Dennis Ramsay, who, born on July 3, 1808, and named after the family's late good friend and neighbor, lived well into the present century and often regaled his descendants with an account of the event during his later years.

At the time of his visit to Alexandria, Lafayette would have been crowding seventy—by no means too old to remember the happenings of half a century earlier, when he had visited the United States for the first time. It would thus have been at least theoretically possible for the custodian of the eagle to have collected at firsthand most of the other information contained in this book, which actually derives from somewhat less direct sources. In other words, although we are now about to celebrate its bicentennial, the American Revolution may not be quite so deeply concealed in the past as the history books cause it to appear. Times change, to be sure, but not perhaps quite as suddenly as we sometimes like to imagine. One's own seniority has, of course, some bearing on this matter. The slightly paradoxical rule seems to be that, for someone old enough to regard the Revolution as only three or four lifetimes in the past, the war will seem more recent than it does to a person for whom two centuries comprise a lifetime multiplied by ten or twenty.

Just as the laws of perspective in drawing enable an artist to create the illusion that an object drawn on a flat sheet of paper has three dimensions, analogous tricks of historical perspective can sometimes serve to give the past a substantiality which it would otherwise lack. Through them, we may sometimes enjoy the illusion of sharing the motives and responses of historical personages as completely as we do those of our own contemporaries. When this occurs, we often find disconcertingly vivid similarities between their age and our own. We can, for example, comprehend that, to many members of the British public in the late eighteenth century, the American Revolution must have seemed a distant and irrelevant struggle in which they really had no substantial stake. Opinions in the United States were likewise sharply divided and often completely reversible. Benedict Arnold and his pretty bride, the former Peggy Shippen, were by no means the only ones who changed sides during the war—and monetary gain was by no means the only incentive even in their case.

Efforts by any historian to draw parallels between events of the past and those of the present are likely to be not only gratuitous but open to immediate challenge. Nonetheless, at the risk of seeming to endorse this fallacy, it may be permissible also to recall that, to his own contemporaries, Washington must have appeared in a totally different light from that of historical hindsight. That many of the most astute men of his age viewed him with considerable alarm was entirely natural and understandable. They were quite unaware that after two terms as President he would be revered by posterity as the Father of his Country—or even that his country would ever have such a thing as a president. What worried them, on the contrary, was the distinctly unpleasant possibility that they might be exchanging the distasteful rule of George III for that of some homespun Virginian Cromwell. This was a prospect that held small charm for New Englanders and others who felt that they had little in common with such tidewater aristocrats to begin with.

Another related point concerns the state of colonial society in general. Everyone knows that, whether they came from England, Holland, France, or Spain, most of the colonists in the Western Hemisphere were drawn from the ranks of the underprivileged in their former homes. What is less generally stressed is that by the time of the Revolution the first century and a half of American history had provided ample opportunity for a thorough restructuring and reclassification of society in the New World settlements. In most of these, the rebels were naturally not to be found among those who had done well for themselves in their new environment. These latter, being anxious to preserve their advantages by maintaining the *status quo*, were much more likely to be Tories—i.e. conservatories— of whom some three thousand were evacuated from Boston alone during the first year of the war, and many thousands more from New York, Philadelphia, and the South later on. Some of these unhappy refugees fled to Nova Scotia or Newfoundland, others to the Bahamas, and others all the way home to the British Isles.

The eventual effect of their departure was to leave the new United States to be developed by a society from which the "better elements" had been strained off twice, first by the original migration in which these elements had been left behind and second by the war itself, which skimmed off much of whatever upper crust had developed in the interim. Meanwhile, the Revolution was conducted mainly by members of a class which, if not the dregs of society, at least, with a few exceptions, had little in common with the Virginia grandees who had joined the rebellion for reasons of their own which were quite different from those of their Northern allies. Most of the New Englanders and those of the wavering central states viewed the Southerners, Washington included, as affluent, landproud snobs, while the Virginians, in their turn, had little use for the "leveling" tendencies of their Northern allies.

The purpose of this book, however, is not to emphasize these aspects of the struggle, let alone to reinterpret them according to the crotchets of our own time. Rather, it is to bring into a somewhat sharper focus than that in which we usually consider them some of the events of those few months in 1777 and 1778 when most of the issues still hung in the balance. In it too I have tried to show in some detail the interplay of character and context that determined the outcome; and to re-create in some measure the scene in which the incongruously low-key climax of the struggle actually took place.

Valley Forge State Park, comprising the area on which George Washington and his bedraggled army spent the winter of 1777–1778, is now a well-groomed tourist attraction of international renown. A dozen or so of the old stone houses where the commander in chief and his generals were quartered have been carefully preserved, along with the little one-room schoolhouse, built in 1705, which was used by the army as a hospital and surgery. Replicas of the log huts occupied by the soldiers stand along the cleared hillsides, as do remnants of the old fortifications. These include the Star Redoubt on top of the central hill and several reconstructed abatis—barricades of treetops and sharp branches set up, like barbed wire in more recent times, to impede attack—protecting the sites of the old gun emplacements.

A handsome chapel and an impressive memorial arch face each other across the green expanse of what the British historian, Sir George Otto Trevelyan, called "the most celebrated encampment in the world's history." In the spring, pink dogwood trees—a special strain developed by park botanists—bloom in the wooded hills that fringe the grassy slopes. Every year, a million or more visitors come there to revere the memory of the months that marked the turning point of the Revolution.

The establishment of Valley Forge Park took place only in 1903, but the first visitor to the area arrived more than a hundred years before that. He was "an elderly person of dignified appearance dressed in a plain suit of black" who reined in his horse on the Gulph Road near where some farmers were plowing, dismounted, and walked toward them across the fields. The stranger in black asked them a few questions about the old camp, whereupon one of the farmers, a former North Carolinian named Henry Woodman, said that he himself had been at Valley Forge with the army. At this, the elderly gentleman expressed a lively interest and replied that he had been there too. His name, he added, was George Washington.

Woodman apologized for not recognizing his former commander in chief. The general looked so different in civilian clothes, he said, and of course, a lot of time had passed already. The two men then fell to reminiscing about the old days, ten years before. . . .

WINTER QUARTERS

1

"THERE IS A hundred times more enthusiasm for this revolution in the first café you choose to name in Paris than there is in all the United States together."

This brusque comment by Colonel Louis le Bèque de Presle du Portail, in one of his first letters home after arriving in the summer of 1777 to serve as chief of engineers of the Colonial Army, summed up the basic problem that confronted its commander in chief in the third year of the war. Even more cogently than in Du Portail's bitter jibe, the nation's disenchantment was expressed by the rudimentary statistics.

Eighty-five years later, in the Civil War, the South, with a white population of some six million, kept an army of four hundred thousand in the field for four years. A proportionate response by the thirteen colonies, with their population of three million, would have been an army of two hundred thousand. Actually, they never managed to muster up more than fifty thousand at any one time, and even this was a paper figure and one which included many thousands of local militia who served intermittently and, as a rule, ineffectively. The real Continental Army never numbered more than twenty thousand, and Washington rarely had more than twelve thousand of these under his direct command. At Valley Forge his roster of effectives at one time dropped to a low of barely five thousand. Even these were often so ill-fed and ill-equipped that many if not most were unfit to carry arms.

Like the number of his troops, their wretched condition

Recruiting poster.

was in large part an indication of the nation's attitude toward the war, as reflected by that revered body, the Continental Congress. Had the same Congress that declared war in 1775, or the one that had passed the Declaration of Independence a year later, remained in session, its delegates might well have learned from increasing experience how to handle a job which, difficult enough to start with, had grown much more so as the war went on. On the contrary, by the autumn of 1777, most of the original group had left to help administer their own states, like Patrick Henry who was now governor of Virginia; to take up some more active civilian role, like John Adams who was presently to join what he called the "militia diplomats" in Paris; or to accept commissions in the army, like Thomas Mifflin, John Sullivan, and Washington himself.

Their replacements at the little town of York, to which Congress had repaired when the British occupied Philadelphia in September, included only two of the members who had voted unanimously for Washington as commander in chief two years before. Few of the new ones had ever even met the commander in chief let alone known him at firsthand, through working with him on committees or chatting with him in the corridors of Independence Hall. What they did know, on the contrary, was the exalted legend that had quickly grown up around him in the subsequent two years, a legend which inclined them to be jealous of his acclaim and eager to display their own authority. Even John Adams, in a characteristically pithy phrase, had advised their predecessors in 1777 to cease worshipping "an image which their own hands have molden," and the present Congress was more than ready to follow his advice.

For the commander in chief himself, it had been a difficult and disappointing year, downhill most of the way from a magnificently promising start. Driven out of Long Island and then New York in the summer and early fall of 1776 by the British under General Sir William Howe, Washington and his disheartened troops had spent the late autumn skulking about the hill country of northern New Jersey, winding up beyond a crook of the Delaware River in the northeast corner of Bucks County, Pennsylvania. From here, famished for anything remotely resembling a victory but faced instead with the likelihood that his dwindling army would disintegrate entirely when most of its soldiers' terms of enlistment ended on New Year's Day, the commander in chief had written candidly to his brother John Augustine: "If every nerve is not strained to recruit the New Army with all possible expedition, I think the game is pretty near up. . . ."

Then he had taken the steps that gave the lie to his own forebodings. The reason the Delaware River afforded him protection of sorts was that he had made sure that all the available river craft—mostly the forty- to sixty-foot canoe-shaped Durham boats used to convey farm produce downriver to, and manufactured goods up from, the colonial capital of Philadelphia—were safely moored on his side. Now, on the short, stormy afternoon of Christmas Day, he used them to ferry his whole army of some twenty-four hundred men back across the ice-strewn

4

stream at a point known as McKonkey's Ferry, some nine miles north of the strong outpost of Trenton, held by Colonel Johann Gottlieb Rall with three regiments of unsuspecting German mercenaries from the princedom of Hesse-Cassel. Rall spent the evening at a Christmas party drinking and playing cards at the house of a hospitable villager named Abraham Hunt. During the evening, a Tory farmer from Bucks County came to the door with a note to tell him that Washington's army was crossing the river. A black servant handed Rall the note, but the colonel, too engrossed in his game to be bothered, stuffed it in his pocket to be looked at later.

In the battle for Trenton that started at eight the next morning, Rall got his death wound within the first hour. When he was carried into his headquarters, the aide who removed his uniform put his hand into the vest pocket, pulled out the crumpled piece of paper, and gave it to the colonel. Rall now looked at it and said: "If I had read this at Mr. Hunt's, I wouldn't be here." Those were almost his last words. Death at least spared him the embarrassment of the subsequent inquiry conducted by his sovereign, the Margrave of Hesse-Cassel. What mostly concerned His Serene Highness was the loss of fifteen regimental flags, an unheard of humiliation which could be expected to diminish the market value of the troops upon which he depended heavily for the upkeep of his court. Along with the standards, Rall had lost most of his men, the Battle of Trenton, and, with it, as things finally turned out, quite possibly the whole war as well.

Trenton was a major victory, and the first real one of

the war for the rebel army, but even that was not the brightest event that marked the turn of the year for Washington. Knowing that this would be followed promptly by the dispersal of his seasoned troops, he recrossed the river to rest them for a few days, resolved to put all he had on the line in one more throw of the dice while he still had them in his hand. On the thirtieth of the month, he lined up his men, rode out in front of the line, and promised a bonus of ten dollars in addition to their regular pay to any who would volunteer to stay on with the army for another six weeks. No one stood forward to accept. The general had to repeat his offer, this time begging them to believe that if they left him now the war would be over and lost despite the victory at Trenton. He stopped speaking and waited again. This time first a few men, then more, then most, reluctantly stepped forward. Enough finally stayed on—about twelve hundred—to give him the nucleus of an army for a few weeks more.

With this handful, backed by about a thousand new militiamen, Washington had crossed the river once more on New Year's Day. In Trenton again, he waited until General Lord Charles Cornwallis, hastily dispatched from New York to command the strong garrison at Princeton, marched the twelve miles between the two villages to take advantage of what looked like a wildly overconfident move on the part of his enemy. Whether Washington had planned his riposte in advance or whether he was merely counting on Cornwallis to do something that would give him a chance to improvise another stunning surprise, no one has ever been quite sure. Washington, who kept a diary throughout most of his life except—lest it fall into enemy hands—during the war years, never wrote down his reasons and never explained them. The memorable words on this occasion came from his opponent. After a second bitterly contested battle in the streets of Trenton, Cornwallis had him pinned against the river and said gaily as darkness fell and the day's fighting ended: "We've got the old fox safe now. We'll . . . bag him in the morning."

When morning came, the old fox had dodged out of reach of Cornwallis' bag—and far down the road toward the now sparsely manned garrison at Princeton. By midday, his troops had taken Nassau Hall, then the biggest building in the whole of North America, and Washington had won his second smashing victory within nine days. This one put an irremediable gap in the long line of British forts strung out across the state which was meant to split the colonies in half and thus ensure the fall of Philadelphia at the invaders' convenience. All in all, the two battles comprised an amazing achievement and one that, as the news of them spread, produced the intended result of giving the colonies renewed faith in eventual victory.

In offering his men a ten-dollar bonus, Washington had exceeded any authority given him by Congress; if worse came to worst, he would have had to pay it out of his own pocket or with whatever he could borrow. But even before he had time to explain his action, pointing out that there was no other way to keep the army alive, Congress, meeting at Baltimore on the twenty-seventh, had voted him in so many words the power to do exactly what he had already done. This was "to use every endeavor, by giving bounties and otherwise, to prevail upon the troops whose time of enlistment shall expire at the end of this month to stay with the Army so long after that period as its situation shall render their stay necessary."

Awake at last to dire reality, Congress had also gone on to vest in him authority to raise, or try to raise, sixteen additional battalions of infantry, three thousand light horse, three regiments of artillery, and a corps of engineers, and to establish their pay, along with other forms of civil authority which amounted to making him, for a term of six months, a military dictator. The enabling resolution, moreover, was forwarded to the commander in chief with a covering letter which said: "Happy it is for this country that the General of their forces can safely be entrusted with the most unlimited power and neither personal security, liberty or property be in the least endangered thereby." On his return visit to Trenton, with more than half of the same troops who had made the crossing on Christmas night, Washington had taken time on New Year's Day to acknowledge the honor with a graceful letter in which he said that, "as the sword was the last resort for the preservation of our liberties, so it ought to be the first to be laid aside when those liberties are firmly established."

But while, in the ensuing months, the army had never quite descended to the dismal state of Christmas Day, 1776, the brisk pace of the eight days that followed was not one that could long be maintained. After a dreary winter in the hills behind Morristown, New Jersey, the spring and summer brought a renewal of the uneasy defensive maneuvering of the year before. News of a new British Army on the way south from Quebec under General John Burgoyne raised the strong likelihood that Howe would try to go up the Hudson to join him. Instead, unaccountably, Howe took his army to sea in the fleet commanded by his brother, Admiral Lord Richard Howe, and was next reported off Cape May on the Delaware coast. Then, as suddenly as it had appeared, the great fleet—observers onshore counted 228 sailing vessels— vanished over the horizon. Had this been a feint to draw Washington south while the British Army sailed north again, bound for the Hudson and a juncture with Burgoyne? Or did the Howes plan to land the army somewhere even farther to the south for an independent attack on Philadelphia, while Burgoyne worked down from Canada?

Never quite sure what to expect, Washington's course was clarified somewhat when Admiral Howe's fleet reappeared at the entrance to Chesapeake Bay, apparently intending now to land the troops as far up as they could be moved by water. Leaving it to General Horatio Gates, with Benedict Arnold and Arthur St. Clair as top field commanders, to deal with Burgoyne in the north, Washington hurried southward to try to fend off Howe's assault on the capital, some fifty miles north of his landing. On the way, he took the opportunity of marching his army through Philadelphia so as to give its citizens a good look at their defenders.

The result was by no means an unmitigated success. Although the baggage train and camp followers, including the camp women, had prudently been instructed to take a circuitous route around the city, and although the men, mostly in hunting shirts and overalls, were dressed as well as they could manage with bright sprigs of green in their hats, observers who watched the two-hour line march past could find obvious faults in it, like those discerned by the captious John Adams: "Much remains yet to be done. Our soldiers have not yet, quite the Air of Soldiers. They dont step exactly in Time. They dont hold up their Heads, quite erect, nor turn out their Toes, exactly as they ought. They dont all of them cock their Hats—and such as do, dont all wear them the same Way."

What followed the parade a fortnight later was the disheartening encounter with Howe and Cornwallis at Brandywine Creek, where they contrived what was tactically a replay of the Battle of Long Island a year before. While a relatively small force of German mercenaries held Washington's attention by threatening to cross the stream at a place called Chadds Ford, they took their main body to a ford farther up the small river and crossed it to swing around on the rebels' right flank. Washington had finally discerned what was happening just in time to avoid a complete route like that of the year before, but not in time to escape a damaging defeat. Their victory put the British in position to move into the capital on September 26 without much further fighting.

The loss of Philadelphia, while a serious blow, made less difference now than it would have a year earlier; and by the time it fell, Congress had had time to move, first to Lancaster and then to York. Meanwhile, still buoyed up by the knowledge that the British had been beaten before and could be again, Washington's troops, having rested and regrouped, felt confident enough by October 4 to launch an attack on Howe's main encampment three miles outside the capital in the suburb of Germantown. Washington's plan for this engagement called for three separate forces to approach the camp by night marches along three different roads, whereupon they would launch a simultaneous surprise attack which might conceivably wipe out the main British army and end the war. The complexity of maneuver combined with precise timing required for the execution of this scheme would have taxed the competence of a far more seasoned and well-drilled force than the mixed bag of some ten thousand Continentals and militia under Washington's command at the time. Not surprisingly, it failed to work—in part because, just when victory looked possible, two elements of the rebel forces which were actually in the process of closing a pincer movement mistook each other for enemy. They began to exchange fire so vigorously that each fell back, thus triggering a confused retreat that soon became general.

The vigor with which his troops had fought at Germantown and the apparently narrow margin by which his plan had miscarried served to some extent to qualify the commander in chief's disappointment in its result. It also had resounding effects elsewhere, for, as Trevelyan was to write in a well-considered appraisal more than a century later: "Eminent generals and statesmen of sagacity, in every European court, were profoundly impressed by learning that a new army, raised within the year, and undaunted by a series of recent disasters, had assailed a vigorous enemy in its own quarters and only been repulsed after a sharp and dubious conflict. . . ."

Nonetheless, taken as a whole, the first nine months of the year showed a debit rather than a credit balance to the account of the commander in chief. Just where this left him in mid-October was brought forcibly to his attention by a curious incident that occurred on the fifteenth of the month, in the form of a call at his headquarters in White Marsh, a few miles north of Philadelphia, by a highly respectable not to say distinguished resident of that city which was then one of the four or five biggest in the English-speaking world. Her name was Mrs. Elizabeth Graeme Ferguson.

Daughter of a leading Philadelphia physician and wife of a well-known citizen—who had, however, welcomed Howe's arrival at the capital—Mrs. Ferguson's purpose in calling on the commander in chief was to deliver in person a fourteen-page letter from a personage of considerable renown. This was the Reverend Jacob Duché, whose impeccable credentials as a believer in the colonial cause went back to the seventh of September, 1774. This was the day on which a report—later proved erroneous—had reached Congress that the British forces occupying Boston were bombarding the town. In the interests of religious unity, a minister of the Established Church had been invited to open the proceedings, and Mr. Duché did so by reading the Psalm appointed for the day, the 35th, which started with the resounding verses:

> Plead thou my cause, O Lord, with them that strive with me: and fight thou against them that fight against me.
> Lay hand upon the shield and buckler: and stand up to help me.

Bring forth thy spear, and stop the way against them that persecute me: say unto my soul, I am thy salvation.

Of this opening, John Adams noted: "It seemed as if Heaven had ordained that Psalm to be read on that morning." From it, the clergyman had gone on to an eloquent prayer of his own composition which, according to the same authority, "filled every Bosom." When it developed the next day that what the report of the bombardment really referred to was merely the seizure of the powder magazine at Charlestown, this appeared to many delegates as a providential answer to the Reverend Duché's apt solicitations.

Eager to see what this staunch patriot now had to say under the stress of the enemy occupation of his own city, Washington must have found the contents of the Duché letter disconcerting to say the least. Casting himself in the role of a divinely inspired peacemaker, what its author proposed was that Washington prevail upon Congress to revoke the Declaration of Independence and start peace negotiations at once. Duché felt certain that such a move would have wide backing in the colonies. If Congress proved recalcitrant, said its former chaplain, "you have an infallible recourse still left: negotiate for your country as the head of your Army." In proposing this dramatic road to reconciliation, he proved as articulate on paper as he had been in the pulpit:

Take an impartial view of the present Congress, and what can you expect from them? . . . These are not the men you engaged to serve; these are not the men that America has chosen to represent her. Most of them were chosen by a little, low faction, and the few gentlemen that are among them now are well known to lie on the balance, and looking up to your hand alone to turn the beam. 'Tis you, sir, and you only that support the present Congress; of this you must be fully sensible.

On the subject of the army, the eminent prelate was even more explicit:

The whole world knows that its very existence depends upon you; that your death or captivity disperses it in a moment, and that there is not a man on that side the question in America, capable of succeeding you. As to the Army itself, what have you to expect from them? Have they not frequently abandoned even yourself in the hour of extremity? Have you, can you have, the least confidence in a set of undisciplined men and officers, many of whom have been taken from the lowest of the people, without principle, without courage? Take away them that surround your person, how few are there that you can ask to sit at your table!"

Leaving out the gratuitous snobbery of the last clause, there was considerable truth in all this. Given Washington's position as the leader of a few forlorn and diminished regiments in an unpopular war backed by an unsympathetic and woefully incompetent government, the line of action proposed by Duché might well have had some appeal for him—had he been a different sort of person. Being the sort of person he was, he did not bother to

14

reply to the letter but merely sent it on to Congress without comment.

That Washington might well have chosen the course proposed by his no doubt sincere and well-motivated correspondent seems in retrospect entirely inconceivable. This may in itself be the most formidable testimony to the extraordinary character of this enigmatic figure, who nowadays seems so remote and even alien to a world grown inured to accepting the dictates of expediency, or self-interest. Washington's was a character formed to meet the predicament in which he found himself, precisely as though he had indeed been molded especially for the purpose by what he himself—a Deist though he never took Communion—was pleased to describe, with due humility, as Providence.

2

ACCORDING TO ONE of. George Washington's renowned biographers, the Reverend Mason L. Weems, the key event of his subject's childhood took place when, given a miniature ax, he promptly used it to hack down an imported English cherry tree. Questioned by his father about this act of vandalism, small George is reported to have disarmed parental wrath with the somewhat self-righteous answer:

"I can't tell a lie, Pa; you know I can't tell a lie. I did cut it with my little hatchet."

For a century or more after its appearance in the Weems biography, this edifying anecdote was almost as much a part of the American credo as the preamble to the Declaration of Independence. Consequently when, in the nineteen twenties and thirties, it became fashionable to deride all such heroic legends, historians naturally felt called upon to reexamine this one. On the demonstrable premises that Parson Weems was often careless in his research and that he was also the only source for the incident in question, they concluded that it was complete fabrication.

Actually, the findings submitted by the debunking historians may well be just as erroneous as Weems's. While Weems often exaggerated, he obviously lacked the specialized bent required for the creation of pure fiction. George's father, Augustine, a prosperous tobacco farmer and accomplished surveyor, was just the sort of landed proprietor who might well have imported his cherry trees from England; and to give a mid-eighteenth-century Virginia boy an ax or a hatchet was surely no stranger than to give a contemporary one a space helmet. The chopping itself is much more plausible than many of the things that Washington ascertainably accomplished later on; and it seems fairly safe to say that, whether or not the cherry tree incident ever occurred, let alone precisely as related by Weems, a good many others of similar import must have done so in view of what appears to have been the major activating strain in young Washington's character throughout boyhood and adolescence. This is what specialists in such matters nowadays describe as a "father identification"; and while recourse to such clinical jargon is normally to be avoided, its use in this case may be excusable, provided both author and reader know exactly what is meant by it.

Nowadays when, for reasons which need not be enumerated here, so many youths seem to be in lively revolt not only against their male parents but against all sources of authority or even responsibility including that vague entity known as "the Establishment," a term like "father identification" may well seem to denote some rare and sinister abnormality, if not indeed an actual derangement. In fact, all it really means is that its possessor was what was known in an earlier and simpler era as "a dutiful son." There was nothing whatever abnormal or alarming about this. Sons then were usually equipped with male parents who, instead of dashing off at the wheel of some mechanical marvel to a distant and mysterious "office," there to engage in a magical process known as "making a living," stayed at home to do interesting and companionable things like farming. By the time sons reached adolescence, or even earlier, they were thus frequently able to get on terms of intimate cordiality not only with their fathers, but also, by corollary, with many other older persons, instead of regarding them all as alien curiosities to be flouted, sneered at, or ignored.

Where Washington differed from his contemporaries in this respect was chiefly that he got the point even sooner and more completely than most. For example, nothing could have been more natural for a youth in his position than to follow his father's footsteps into the sideline profession of surveying. What was unusual in his case was that he did it when his father was no longer on hand to influence or help him. In doing so, moreover, he utilized his father's own instruments, in the form of a handsome leather-bound surveyor's kit which he had inherited on the latter's death, when he himself was only eleven.

For a well-connected young man in eighteenth-century Virginia, where land amounted almost to a form of currency, surveying was a pursuit comparable in popularity to banking or mutual fund management nowadays. It was also, in an unmapped countryside and in an era when warfare depended much more than it does now upon topical features, an invaluable basis for subsequent employment in the then even more fashionable field of war. Washington's military debut was, to be sure, delayed until he reached the age of twenty, but his spontaneous identification with the sources of authority—then as now a *sine qua non* for the subsequent assumption of responsibility and command—had been demonstrated long before that. Most of the closest early associations of the future "father of his country" were with men who were not only older than himself but the possessors of superior prestige and power. The first of these was naturally his own half brother, Lawrence, fourteen years his senior, who, as the eldest son of Augustine and his first wife, had become the heir, not to a mere set of surveyor's tools, but to the 2500-acre Washington tobacco farm on the Potomac River.

Schooled at Appleby, England, Lawrence Washington had returned to Virginia in time to serve under Admiral Edward Vernon in the glamorous expedition to Cartagena that climaxed the famous "War of Jenkins's Ear." Then, after Augustine Washington's death in 1743, he settled down with his attractive bride, the former Anne Fairfax, on the inherited estate which he named in honor of his former commanding officer. Young George, who grew up on the much smaller family farm where his mother continued to live after her husband's death, often went to visit at Mount Vernon. At sixteen, he was already proficient enough as a surveyor to make himself doubly welcome by being of occasional use to his approving host, who in due course invited him to stay on as long as he liked.

Lawrence Washington's young wife was the daughter of a well-to-do neighbor named Colonel William Fairfax, a cousin of the Lord Thomas Fairfax whose five-and-a-half-million-acre domain—later to be divided up into twenty-one counties—made him the colony's largest proprietor. When Lord Fairfax arrived from London at the age of fifty-four to take up residence thereon, young Washington came to know him well but it was the colonel who became the second of what psychiatrists might call his paternal substitutes. One bond between the two was a common enthusiasm for fox hunting, for which Washington, already a fine horseman, showed precocious aptitude. Another was their understandable curiosity about the extensive portion of the Fairfax holdings that lay unmapped behind the Blue Ridge Mountains in the Shenandoah Valley. When his lordship decided to have the whole area surveyed, Colonel Fairfax arranged for Washington—along with George Fairfax, Anne Washington's younger brother—to become a member of the team that performed the job, under an experienced superintendent.

Washington's execution of his part in this formidable assignment was such as to cause his mentor, on its completion, to recommend him for the lucrative post of official surveyor of Culpeper County to which, after a brief refresher course in the capital at Williamsburg, he was duly appointed. Within three years, before he had yet reached his majority, young Washington had acquired two thousand acres of promising farmland on his own account. In that same year he received a sudden addition to these holdings which vastly enhanced his status as well as his wealth.

Along with a contagious enthusiasm for martial exploits, Lawrence Washington had brought back with him from the siege of Cartagena the germ of tuberculosis of the lungs, as a remedy for which in 1751 his doctors recommended a stay in Barbados. One proof of reciprocal affection for his visiting half brother was that Lawrence invited him to go along on the trip—which proved to be Lawrence's last, and George's sole, excursion outside the continent of North America. Even stronger evidence was that, when Lawrence Washington came home to die in 1752, his will made George Washington one of those responsible for his estate as trustee for his widow and her small daughter. When the daughter also soon after fell ill and expired, Washington became in effect the proprietor of Mount Vernon—for her half interest in which he eventually paid Anne a substantial lump sum as a more dependable source of the yearly income to which she was entitled. Aided by this handsome inheritance, he also acquired his half brother's military title as one of the four adjutant generals of the colony. This appointment, in which Washington launched his career as a soldier, carried with it the rank of major, the duty of drilling the local militia, and a stipend of 100 pounds a year.

Third and most consequential of Washington's relationships with substitute fathers of whom he became the beneficiary was the one which presently developed with Governor Robert Dinwiddie, to whom he had been favorably mentioned both by Lord Fairfax and his cousin, the colonel. During the years when young Washington had been getting started as a surveyor, trouble had been brewing on the western frontier between French voyageurs who had already reached the Ohio Valley from the north via the St. Lawrence River, and British pioneers who were now approaching it through the agency of the Ohio Company, from the south via the Allegheny River. By the autumn of 1753, Dinwiddie felt that the time had come to scare the French off by warning them that "it is a matter of equal Concern and Surprize to me to hear that a Body of French Forces are erecting Fortresses and making Settlements upon that River within his Majesty's Dominions." When the question arose as to who should be entrusted with the tricky chore of delivering this stern missive to the French at Fort

LeBoeuf—five hundred miles away, on the site of what is now Waterford, Pennsylvania—the governor naturally thought of Washington, as a young man who knew the frontier country, whose rank justified the selection, and with whom by now he was directly acquainted not only as a protégé of Colonel Fairfax but also as a government appointee. When, at a meeting in Williamsburg on the thirty-first of October, Washington offered to deliver the message in person, the governor accepted on the spot. Washington characteristically got started the same day, taking with him a guide, an interpreter, and a small retinue of servants.

Washington's mission to Fort LeBoeuf, from which he brought back the report that the French had every intention of staying on the Ohio, was the first move in what historians later called the French and Indian War. The second occurred when Governor Dinwiddie made him deputy commander of a force of some six hundred men whose assignment was to occupy a fort that had been built by the Ohio Company at the junction of the Allegheny and Monongahela rivers. Sent out with the advance detachment, Washington found that the French had already occupied the fort and had no intention of giving it up. While pondering what to do next, he and his 150 men, informed by Indian scouts of the presence of a party of thirty-two Frenchmen in the nearby woods, surprised them by night, killing ten, including their commander and taking the rest prisoner. Enraged, the main body of the French emerged from their stronghold, surrounded Washington's force, and, after a nine-hour siege of their makeshift "Fort Necessity," forced them to surrender.

The engagement between Washington's detachment

and the French scouting party—which, according to French accounts of the affair, was bringing dispatches under a flag of truce—got the war that was to serve as the prologue to the American Revolution started in earnest. The next development occurred the following year when General Edward Braddock, a seasoned British commander in his mid-fifties, arrived in Virginia to lead an army of five thousand men against the major French stronghold of Fort Duquesne, later to be Fort Pitt and finally Pittsburgh. Much impressed by Washington—by this time a strikingly handsome young officer, well over six feet tall and the most celebrated frontier soldier in the colony—Braddock promptly made him an aide-de-camp with the courtesy rank of colonel. In this predictable capacity Washington became the sole hero of the smashing defeat which Braddock suffered on July 9, 1755, along with the wounds of which he died two days later, after bequeathing his favorite horse to Washington.

During the next two years, despite their temporary advantage, the French were gradually obliged to withdraw their forces to Quebec where the British eventually won the war in 1759 when Wolfe, ably assisted by a gallant young captain named Sir William Howe, defeated Montcalm. Meanwhile Washington—in effect commander in chief of the armed forces of a semiautonomous state in his early twenties—upheld Virginia's position on the frontier until November of 1758, when he marched back to Fort Duquesne and found it deserted. Shortly thereafter he withdrew from active service to enjoy a conqueror's reward by marrying an attractive young widow named Martha Dandridge Custis, then reputedly one of the richest women in

Virginia, and taking up the life of a prosperous fox-hunting squire on his increasingly commodious plantation.

George Washington's brief but spectacular career in the French and Indian War was one of the things that qualified him for his later post as commander in chief of the Continental Army in 1775. Another and, as events proved, perhaps even more important qualification was what he did in the sixteen-year interim. When the war ended, so far as Virginia was concerned, with the fall of Fort Duquesne, Washington stood for election to the House of Burgesses as the member from Frederick County. Campaigning in absentia, on the strength of his military record and with the backing of the Fairfax clan, he won handily with 309 votes to 239 for his closest rival.

The House of Burgesses resembled a modern state legislature with one important difference: each colony was wholly independent of the others and responsible only to the Crown. Washington's membership required his presence for only a month or so every year, and there is no record of his making important forensic contributions to a body which also included among its members such prodigies in eloquence as Patrick Henry and Thomas Jefferson. What was more to the point, however, was that, the less active part he took in debate, the better chance he had to study not only the merits of the dispute with George III that developed during those years but also the peculiarities of parliamentary behavior in general and of the House of Burgesses in particular. Thus when the time came for Virginia to send a delegation to the first Con-

tinental Congress in 1774, he was one of the seven delegates dispatched from the most prosperous of the thirteen
colonies. In that Congress and the one that met the next
year, after the Revolution had started at Lexington and
Concord, Washington had as little to say as he had had
in the House of Burgesses, but he worked congenially
with its members, of whom all soon came to know him
well at least by sight. In addition to being the tallest man
in the hall, Washington in 1775 was also the only one
in uniform, which he wore as a means of suggesting—
consciously or otherwise, but more clearly than even an
accomplished orator could have done in words—the action called for and the role in it appropriate for himself.

A point worth noting here is a fundamental difference
in viewpoint which appears to have existed between the
two leading colonies of Massachusetts and Virginia in
their mutual antipathy toward the British Crown. The
Northerners were essentially middle-class merchants or
small-parcel farmers whose original migration to the New
World had been motivated primarily by a desire to escape
religious persecution. To them, George III appeared in
the role of an ogreish tyrant who meant to grind them
beneath his heel. The Southerners, on the contrary, were
often the descendants of well-to-do if not wealthy county
families, and their overseas holdings in the tidewater
country of Virginia had already made them the equals in
affluence of many peers of the realm at home. What they
resented about George III, much as such peers might
have done under comparable conditions, was his impudence in daring to impinge upon their privileges as
members of a proud and self-sufficient aristocracy.

Washington's military record as an officer of field grade who had not only served as second-in-command to a senior British general, but also later commanded a six-hundred-man army of his own was in itself enough to make him militarily the best qualified colonial candidate for commander in chief. His political preparation as a member of both the House of Burgesses and the Continental Congress made him the only man on either side, with the possible exception of Sir William Howe, by now a celebrated British general, who could claim legislative as well as martial experience. It was, however, neither one of these outstanding qualifications nor even the unique combination of both that caused him to be selected for the post. The cause was the apparently much less relevant fact that he owned a plantation on the Potomac.

In a war sponsored primarily by the Bostonian merchants, their leading representative, John Adams, had shrewdly perceived that what the colonies needed for commander in chief was a Southerner to give the cause geographical cohesion and an aristocrat to make it socially acceptable. Adams also noted that in Washington—unlike John Hancock, who suspected until the end of his fellow townsman's nominating speech that he himself was the subject of it—both of these requirements were also combined to perfection. When the matter came to a vote the next day, the unanimous concurrence of his colleagues in this view was thus more a tribute to Adams' acute political insight than to Washington's proven capabilities as a statesman and a soldier.

The grave discrepancy between Washington's intrinsic qualifications for his job and the extraneous political reasons for which he had been awarded it became strikingly evident during the next two years. In 1775, by his successful siege of Boston, and later by his victories at Trenton and Princeton, Washington had demonstrated his capacities as a field commander dramatically enough to make him a hero both to the nation as a whole and to the troops who served under him. To Adams and others, for whom his purpose had been largely served as soon as he accepted his post, the extent to which thereafter he became a national hero made him not merely a liability but a positive threat. Meanwhile, however, they were prevented from voicing their alarm by the fact that they could propose nobody else to put in his place; and it was not until the fall of 1777 that Washington's position as commander in chief, contrary to the assertions of the Reverend Duché, became suddenly and seriously vulnerable.

What caused the abrupt change was, of course, the great colonial victory at Saratoga on October 17, making Horatio Gates, to whom this tremendous achievement was attributed, immediately the man of the hour. In response to his own personal communication of this triumph, Congress proclaimed December 18 a day of national thanksgiving for reasons which John Adams summed up in a characteristic letter to his wife. The proclamation was justified, he explained, precisely because the victory had not been due "to the Commander in Chief, nor to the southern Troops. If it had been, Idolatry, and Adulation would have been unbounded; so excessive as to endanger our Liberties. . . . Now We can allow a certain Citizen to be wise, virtuous, and good, without thinking him a Deity or a saviour."

Notice of the thanksgiving proclamation reached Washington at Gulph Mills, Pennsylvania, where his army was in temporary camp. Far from suspecting the growing hostility that lay behind it, the commander in chief issued General Orders postponing the departure that had been scheduled for the next day and directing instead "that the army remain in its present quarters and that the Chaplains perform divine service with their special corps and brigades . . . [The Commander] earnestly exhorts, all officers and soldiers, whose absence is not indispensably necessary, to attend with reverence the solemnities of the day."

So far as the troops at Gulph Mills were concerned, there was little in their immediate circumstances to be thankful for. Some days earlier, in response to rumors of an impending British attack on the previous camp at White Marsh, the tents and baggage had been sent north for safekeeping. Since then the men had been sleeping in the open, many of them without blankets and for the past two nights in intermittent snow. Now the baggage train had rejoined the army and the snow had changed to a freezing rain, but the men were still cold, ragged, and hungry. Provisions in camp were so sparse that for many the fare for the thanksgiving dinner, as meager as it was inappropriate, consisted, according to a young Connecticut private named Joseph Plumb Martin,* of "half a gill of rice and a tablespoon full of vinegar"—the latter being the then accepted antidote for scurvy. The day after this frugal celebration, the army set off on the last day's march to Valley Forge. Even if Washington had fully understood what was

* See Appendix I.

going on in Congress, he would have had little time to dwell
on it thereafter.

During the preceding weeks, plans for the winter had
been the subject of lively discussion at staff meetings held
to consider the various alternatives. Much of the boldest
of these was an attack on Philadelphia, a prospect which
naturally appealed to some bellicose elements in Congress. Well aware that anything of this kind was totally
impractical, owing to shortages of everything from man-
power to shoe leather, Washington nonetheless submitted
the proposal to a council of war on November 24, at
which eleven out of fifteen generals voted against it and
gave their reasons in writing. Another was a camp in or
near Wilmington, but this too had both political and tactical disadvantages; the country was flat and hard to for-
tify, it was too far from supply bases, and it left all of the
influential state of Pennsylvania fully exposed to the
enemy.

When the state legislature sent him a resolution to the
effect that the entire area near the capital be safeguarded,
the commander in chief sent back a patient but somewhat
caustic reply: "It would give me infinite pleasure to afford
protection to every individual and to every Spot of
Ground in the whole of the United States. Nothing is
more to my wish. But this is not possible with our present
force." Nonetheless, he gave the argument some weight.
What he needed in short was a site for winter quarters
close enough to Philadelphia to give some degree of protection to the surrounding countryside and at the same

time in itself logistically practical and militarily defensible.

The spot eventually chosen met the requirements better than any other available. Valley Forge, about eighteen miles to the northwest of Philadelphia, was a tiny settlement of a dozen or so fieldstone houses which had grown up around one of the numerous small charcoal furnaces in the iron country of Eastern Pennsylvania. The village stood where a stream called Valley Creek flowed north into the Schuylkill River and the forge itself, with a wheel turned by the creek, was about a mile upstream, almost due south of the junction. For the last two miles of its course, Valley Creek ran through a gorge between two heavily wooded hills known as Mount Joy and Mount Misery. Joy, the hill on the right or eastern bank of the creek, sloped off gradually toward the southeast. With approach from the north side protected by the river and from the west by the Valley Creek gorge, this wide slope formed a natural defensive position—since any attacking force would be fully exposed to fire from the readily fortified area near the crest.

In addition to its inherent tactical virtues, Valley Forge was well situated for Washington's purposes in regard to supplies, to the political requirements of the moment, and to any strategic contingencies that might arise. As to the last, in the event of a forced retreat, he could retire into the mountains of Western Pennsylvania, a region of which he had intimate firsthand knowledge, and wage what would nowadays be called guerrilla war from there. In the absence of such an emergency, Valley Forge provided easy access both to bigger iron towns farther west, where cannon could be refitted during the winter, and to lead mines north of the Schuylkill. Stores of ammunition were accessible from both sources, and the rich Quaker farms on both sides of the Schuylkill would presumably be able to deliver to the army at least some of the produce that would normally have gone into the Philadelphia markets. Finally, by staying within a few miles of the capital, the army would offer some assurance to rebel residents and refugees in the remainder of the state.

To balance these advantages, there were compensating drawbacks. One was that the few substantial houses in the village were nothing like numerous enough to provide billets for all the officers, let alone for the whole army. Another more distressing one was that Howe's army, in the period of skirmishing that had preceded the Battle of Germantown in early October, had burned the forge and destroyed ammunition stores and other supplies that would have been convenient to have had on hand when the army arrived. Still, it was too late now for Washington to do anything about all this; and the decision to move to Valley Forge had been reached in early December.

From Gulph Mills, the route was a section of the broad dirt highway from Philadelphia to Reading known as the Gulph Road. Deep ruts ground into it by farm wagons during the autumn rains were frozen now; their hard ridges, covered with ice or packed snow, made marching difficult even for those of the soldiers who had some sort of footgear. Many, who through the summer and fall had preferred to go barefoot on the then relatively soft surface of the dusty roads, still lacked anything of the sort. Some of these did what they could to repair the lack by wrapping cloths around their feet or making crude moccasins from the untanned hides of the cattle butchered in the camp. Others, whose soles were more toughened or who were unable to acquire even these makeshifts, continued to march barefoot. Private Martin, who had made himself a pair of cowhide slippers, noted that the edges hurt his ankles so much that he wore them only because the alternative "was to go barefoot as hundreds of my companions had to, till they might be tracked by their blood upon the rough frozen ground."

The red tracks on the icy road were also observed by the commander in chief as he rode along in the rear of the troops, and at one point in the march he overtook the officer in command of a regiment to inquire into the matter. The officer explained that there had been an issue of shoes but that the supply had given out before most of his men could get them. For those who had none, there was nothing to do but march without them. "Poor fellows," Washington said, as he watched the barefoot men shuffle quietly past.

In the morning, moving at barely a mile an hour, the army covered six miles to the well-known inn called the King of Prussia. There the troops built fires and warmed up a sparse meal, while the senior officers gathered in the big room on the second floor of the tavern whose signboard showed Frederick the Great in dashing equestrian pose. At four that afternoon, drums beat the signal to fall in, and the early winter twilight turned to darkness as the army covered the last three uphill miles. When they arrived at the bleak, wooded hillside, most of the men, too exhausted even to pitch tents or mount guard, spent the night sitting or lying on the bare ground around log fires.

3

Awake, arouse, Sir Billy!
There's forage in the plain.
Ah! leave your little Filly
And open the campaign.
Heed not a woman's prattle,
Which tickles in the ear,
But give the word for battle,
And grasp the warlike spear.

PURPORTING TO CONVEY to General Sir William Howe the bellicose sentiments of Philadelphia's Tories, these frisky little verses may also shed some light on the activities of the British commander in chief during the winter of 1777–1778. While Washington's condition at Valley Forge was assuredly less comfortable, Sir William's in Philadelphia was in some ways ever more precarious. The enthusiasm he showed for urban frivolities like card games and late suppers at the Indian Queen café were perhaps not so much the casual dissipations of a lazy man as the compulsive compensations of a worried one.

In Boston two years before, Howe had made the acquaintance of a young woman named Mrs. Joshua Loring whose Tory husband was his commissary general for prisoners of war. Described as "a flashing blonde," she had accompanied the army first to New York and then to Philadelphia where it was common knowledge that her real role was that of mistress to the commander in chief. In the capital, they went everywhere together; among their favorite pleasures was the faro bank run by one of Howe's officers, at which Mrs. Loring was reputed to have lost three hundred guineas at a single sitting. Nonetheless, while Howe was indubitably enjoying the reasonably extensive amenities provided by life in Philadelphia, his motives for not opening the campaign may have been more complex than the verse implied.

Like Washington's, Howe's difficulties derived largely from his government—of which, as Member of Parliament for Nottingham, he was himself a minor part. Under George III and his less than inspired prime minister, Lord North, whose thick lips and popeyes, according to Horace Walpole, made him look like a blind trumpet player, Parliament had, to be sure, supported the war in America by substantial majorities. It was also true, however, that a highly articulate minority, including most of the best minds and both of the best speakers of an eloquent age, were vigorously opposed to it. What was especially noteworthy about the faction opposed to the war was that it included not only such renowned spokesmen as Edmund Burke and William Pitt the Elder, now the earl of Chatham, but also the general in charge of prosecuting the hostilities.

That the king, even assuming him to have been as doltish as American schoolbooks would later assert, should have chosen to entrust top command in the war to a general whom he knew to be completely opposed to it seems at first glance incomprehensible. In fact, however, there were at least three compelling reasons for his choice which, when taken together, may have provided ample justification. In the first place, like his brother, Richard, who was Admiral the Viscount Howe, Sir William was the

34

grandson of George I, through his mistress, the Baroness Kilmansegge. Thus he was not only a subject but a cousin, in whom family loyalty if nothing else might well outweigh any ideological scruples he entertained as to the nation's war aims.

In the second place, several of England's other top generals, among them Lord Amherst and Lord Ellingham, were even more strongly opposed than Howe to taking up arms against men at whose side they had fought only a few years before in the hard-won frontier campaigns against their common enemy, the French. And in the third place, in addition to entrusting Howe with command of Britain's armies in the colonies, the government had also given him and his seafaring brother wide latitude to act as peace commissioners. The last assignment, in some respects even more important than his military command, was one for which Sir William Howe's undisguised sympathy for the colonial cause would obviously be an important asset.

To Howe himself the ambiguities of his position had, of course, been painfully apparent from the outset. When the king offered him the post of commander in chief, the general had already promised his Parliamentary constituents, most of whom shared his Whiggish sympathies, that he would refuse to bear arms against the colonials. Much embarrassed by the consequent conflict of loyalties, he then asked his sovereign whether he should consider the offer an invitation or a command. Only when informed that it must be viewed as the latter did he—according to his own account of the matter—reluctantly consent to accept it. His acquiescence, moreover, was obviously moti-

35

vated at least in part by the conviction that his own role in the struggle, after winning a battle or two, would be that of a gallant conqueror, offering generous peace terms.

Howe's sympathy for the colonial cause, while based on the same principles that sustained Burke, Pitt, and their colleagues, was further reinforced both by tactical considerations, which he was better equipped than they to appreciate, and by family tradition. As to the latter, the eldest Howe brother—from whom the admiral had inherited his title and a fortune reputed to be greater than the king's—had died heroically while leading colonial troops against the French at Ticonderoga in 1758; and the monument to his memory in Westminster Abbey had been placed there by grateful New Englanders. As to the former, it was clearer to the general than to most of his Parliamentary colleagues that common sense as well as justice recommended prompt reconciliation between Britain and the colonies. The only alternatives to such an agreement were either full independence or a prolonged occupation; and since simple military arithmetic made it impossible for Britain simultaneously to garrison the whole North American continent and to hold her place as Europe's number one power, the goal in the colonies should be a token victory followed by speedy and honorable peace. As Howe himself phrased it, there seemed to be no reason why both sides should not "sit down like two schoolboys with bloody noses and black eyes" to shake hands and be friends again.

Howe's tactics had from the outset been carefully chosen for compatibility with his dual role. When the rebels dug in at Bunker Hill, their stronghold could read-

*General Sir William Howe, British commander in chief during
the winter of 1778.*

ily have been isolated by landing troops at Charleston Neck, thus cutting off the garrison from its base of supplies. To do so, however, would presumably have had less dramatic impact than the bold stroke of marching straight up the hillside and evicting its defenders at bayonet point, of which Howe had had field command. The bayonet charge had, to be sure, proved more expensive than expected, but nonetheless the gamble had been worthwhile. Howe had later evacuated his army from Boston in the most considerate possible fashion, after explaining to Washington that he had no desire to destroy the city and would not do so if allowed to embark unmolested.

The fighting around New York—at Long Island, Kips' Bay, and Fort Washington, where British buglers had underlined the moral of the affair by blowing calls from the hunting field as the rebels fled across the heights— had, Howe felt, helped to establish the point that colonials could not hope to defeat His Majesty's regulars in an open fight. After Long Island, however, he and his brother had invited the rebel leaders to discuss the possibilities of terms, and the Howe brothers were obviously much miffed when Franklin, who had known them both in England, John Adams, and young Edward Rutledge failed to respond as expected. Nothing to do then but go on fighting a bit longer, but by this time Howe had another hazard to contend with and one which was certainly comparable to the obstacle which Congress represented to his adversary. This was the Ministry of War in London headed by the extraordinary Lord George Germain, whose dubious qualifications for his post included discharge from active military service some years before with the proviso, based on his conduct at the Battle of Minden, that he never again be entrusted with command of troops.

One of the major concerns of the Ministry of War in London during the early winter of 1776–1777 had been a highly readable document entitled "Thoughts for Conducting the War from the Side of Canada," composed by General the Right Honorable John Burgoyne, who had been one of Howe's confreres at Bunker Hill and helped General Guy Carleton raise the seige of Quebec a year later. In this, Burgoyne, who had also demonstrated his literary talents even more convincingly than his military ones by the composition of a successful comedy, argued the merits of an expedition from the fortress of Quebec down the Hudson toward New York. According to Burgoyne, now back in London on furlough, such an expedition could be joined at Albany by Colonel Barry St. Leger, marching eastward from Oswego, and by Howe, sailing up the Hudson from New York. When the three armies met, the rebellion would be split neatly in half and His Majesty's forces could then quell the uprising at their leisure, first in one half and then in the other. This plausible scheme conformed with Lord Germain's own thoughts on the matter to such a degree that, as Burgoyne had obviously intended, he put its author in charge of its execution.

With his pro-colony crony and fellow member of Brooks Club, Charles Fox, Burgoyne placed a hundred-pound bet that he would be back within six months after a victorious campaign. He then sailed for Quebec in the spring of 1777, accompanied by over nine thousand crack

British troops and topnotch German mercenaries. The latter were under the command of Major General Baron Friedrich von Riedesel who brought his wife with him to see the sights, along with their small daughters. In Quebec, before setting off into the wilderness in mid-June, the expedition spent a month or so assembling supplies and equipment, which included, like Howe's army, what appears to have been the customary convenience of a commissary general whose wife also served as mistress to the commander in chief.

The wilderness—of which, except for the waterways of Lake Champlain, Lake George, and the Hudson River, the three hundred miles between Quebec and Albany was almost exclusively composed—was an obstacle which, in concocting his plan, dashing "Gentleman Johnny" Burgoyne, despite his earlier experiences in Canada, had somewhat unaccountably underestimated. That his overdressed and overburdened soldiers finally contrived by midsummer to get within striking distance of their destination was in itself a logistic triumph almost as remarkable in its way as Hannibal's crossing of the Alps. However, by the time it had been achieved, Burgoyne's force was in no condition to win a battle as well, and its resounding defeat at Saratoga was thus perhaps inevitable. What made it even more so was aid to his opponents from the most unlikely source imaginable in the person of the very Lord Germain who had set the whole plan in motion.

Germain's contribution was not related to Burgoyne's basic misconception of the terrain, an error which had in due course been compounded by an unforeseen shortage of baggage animals and by unexpectedly strong opposition which cost him a tenth of his force at the battle of Bennington. It was merely to erase the only point about the whole scheme that was undeniably sound, that is, the projected conjunction of forces which might possibly have enabled the scheme to succeed in spite of all other weaknesses. St. Leger, to be sure, had set out from Oswego with seventeen hundred men, only to be first stopped and then forced to retire at the battles of Oriskany and Fort Stanwix. At New York, on the other hand, Howe, upon whose cooperation the success of the whole enterprise obviously depended, was never even informed that he was expected to take part in it. As a result he not only made no effort to do so, but, at the crucial moment, took his army off to sea in the opposite direction.

If, as Burgoyne expected, Howe had sailed up the Hudson to meet him, the two armies together, even without St. Leger, might well have been competent to crush whatever rebel forces they found between them. Why Howe was never instructed to do so is, accordingly, a point which historians have been debating ever since. That orders to this effect were actually drawn up seems to be well established, and the puzzle is thus merely why they were never sent. The most satisfactory answer appears to be one provided by Lord Shelburne some fifty years later. This was that, when Lord Germain dropped in at the War Office one afternoon to tidy up his desk on his way to the country, the copy of the orders that was being prepared for dispatch to Howe was not yet ready for his signature. Enraged by this example of bureaucratic inefficiency, Germain left without signing it and dismissed the matter from his mind. In any case, his own further comment on the subject was limited to a jaunty memorandum addressed to William Knox, the under secretary of state for the colonies, dated September 29, 1777, when Burgoyne was already within a few days of his disaster:

"I am sorry the Canada army will be disappointed in the junction they expect with Sir William Howe, but the more honor for Burgoyne if he does the business without any assistance from New York."

Howe's decision to proceed by sea from New York to Philadelphia may well have been based at least in part on a suggestion offered by the British-born U.S. deputy commander in chief, General Charles Lee, an old acquaintance who had spent the winter of 1777 as Howe's prisoner in New York. That suggestion was to split the colonies in two by occupying the capital, while leaving his own deputy, Sir Henry Clinton, to hold New York; and it was the inability of Clinton, left with what he called a "damned starved defensive," to come to Burgoyne's assistance when the latter finally appealed to him directly that made the outcome of the pivotal battle of the Revolution, and one later to be included by Edward Shepherd Creasy on his list of the fifteen most decisive battles in the history of the world, a foregone conclusion.

What Howe did finally receive in Philadelphia from his superior in London was a refusal to give him the extensive reinforcements he had asked for in order to carry out the Howe-Lee plan for using the presumably loyalist states of New Jersey, Pennsylvania, and Maryland rather than the Hudson River as a wedge to separate the Northern from the Southern colonies. Thus deprived of ministerial support for a strategy, as sound in its way as Burgoyne's, for

winning a war he did not wish to fight, Howe was understandably upset enough by mid-October of 1777 to request permission to resign. His natural reluctance to
undertake any major offensive moves pending considera-
tion of this request at Whitehall provided further grounds
for his prolonged inaction at Philadelphia, which inspired
not only local versification but a witticism current as far
away as London. This was that Howe should be raised to
the peerage, with the title of Lord Delay Warr.

In Paris, Benjamin Franklin's comment, when informed
that Howe had taken Philadelphia was: "I beg your pardon,
Sir, Philadelphia has taken General Howe." This too was
frequently repeated and it had a basis in fact. Philadelphia
was not only the largest city in the Western Hemisphere but
was certainly the only one in which officers accustomed to
the cozy club and coffeehouse life of London could hope to
find a reasonably congenial equivalent. The capital's famous
assemblies, of the sort which are still being held, were already a tradition of over twenty years' standing. Daughters
of well-to-do Quaker and Tory families soon began to
suffer from what it was considered amusing to call "scarlet
fever," while fashionable hostesses felt no more repugnance
to entertaining Sir William's mistress than they did to the
curious insistence of the Hessian General, Baron Wilhelm
von Knyphausen, upon spreading the butter on his bread
with his thumb instead of with a butter knife. All in all,
life in the capital went along pleasantly enough; and while
there were occasional skirmishes between foraging parties
on the outskirts of the city, the liveliest excitements that

43

Major John André, General Howe's favorite aide-de-camp (a self-portrait).

took place during the winter were amateur theatricals in which the most active participant, as casting director, scene designer, and author of prologues, was Howe's favorite aide-de-camp, Major John André. Among those conspicuously present at these entertainments was likely to be the pretty and precocious seventeen-year-old Peggy Shippen, who twenty years later, when she was Mrs. Benedict Arnold, was called "the handsomest woman in London." Some of André's more graceful verses were addressed to her while others poked fun at Anthony Wayne, the colonial commander who was famous for his daring and far-flung foraging expeditions. By a coincidence, the last installment of André's three-part satiric ballad called "The Cow Chase" would appear in the New York *Royal Gazette* on Saturday, September 23, 1780. This was the same day on which its author was arrested in Tarrytown, New York, just prior to being hanged as a spy for his role in Benedict Arnold's scheme to betray West Point.

By the time Howe finally learned from Lord Germain in April 1778 that his resignation had been accepted, there was clearly neither point nor propriety in jeopardizing an army he was so soon to hand over to his successor, Sir Henry Clinton. There was, however, time enough left for the last and most brilliant of André's *divertissements* and one which, in the doubtless well-founded opinion of that ill-fated young impresario, was "the most splendid entertainment ever given by an army to its General." This was the famous "Mischianza" or Medley, of which the Italian name and style derived from André's earlier period of service in the British garrison at Malta. To provide an appropriate setting for his extravaganza, André had ar-

45

ranged to borrow Walnut Grove, the estate of Thomas Wharton a few miles south of town on the banks of the Delaware. Here British army engineers under Captain John Montresor, for whose services there had been little serious demand, had been called upon to turn the four-acre lawn into the setting for a romanticized replica of a medieval tournament.

The preliminaries to the Mischianza started on the afternoon of May 18 when Howe and his fellow generals were embarked at Knight's Wharf on a fleet of elaborately decorated barges to be rowed downriver in time to regimental music, between banks lined by soldiers on dress parade. On arriving at the designated landing of Old Fort, they walked between rows of saluting grenadiers across the tournament field at the opposite ends of which pavilions had been set up for British and American "Queens of Beauty." After passing under a lofty triumphal arch embellished with a figure of Fame blowing the motto "Tes Lauriers Sont Immortels" from a cardboard trumpet, Howe received a wreathe from a herald who then declaimed a tactful prologue, composed by André:

> "Chained to our arms, while Howe the battle led,
>   Still round these files her wings shall Conquest spread.
>   Loved though he goes, the spirit still remains
>   That with him bore us o'er these trembling plains. . . .
>   Nor fear but equal honors shall repay
>   Each hardy deed where Clinton leads the way."

There followed a competition in which seven "Knights of the Blended Rose," dressed in crimson and white silk and mounted on gray horses, contended against seven "Knights

Peggy Shippen, later Mrs. Benedict Arnold; a pencil portrait by Major John André.

of the Burning Mountain," mounted on black horses and dressed in black and orange, for the favors of fourteen "damsels of honor." The latter included most of Philadelphia's prettiest belles except Peggy Shippen, whose Quaker father thought the whole thing sounded a bit too sophisticated for a teen-ager and kept her at home.

When the fourteen knights had concluded their exercises with swords and lances, the procession re-formed and proceeded to the ballroom of the Wharton house which André had had done up in blue and gold and which was lit by a thousand candles. At ten o'clock there were fireworks on the lawn, and at the stroke of midnight two dozen black waiters in Oriental costume, wearing silver bracelets and collars, served a three-course dinner of four hundred covers while heralds proclaimed toasts to the King, Queen, Army, Navy, Commander, Knights, and Ladies. Dancing continued after supper until four in the morning.

If Howe's inactivity through the five months that preceded the Mischianza remains something of a puzzle to modern historians, they have at least the advantage over Washington in that he lacked clues not only as to what lay behind it, but also as to how long he might expect it to continue. Meanwhile, life on the hillside at Valley Forge presented a vivid contrast to the one which Sir William and his army were enjoying in the captured capital.

4

ON THE MORNING after arriving at Valley Forge, the Colonial Army's most urgent need was shelter. For this, Washington and Du Portail, a much busier engineer-officer than Montresor, had plans in hand. The men were to build a city of a thousand cabins or, in army idiom, "huts" laid out in streets and sections according to the various units. The huts were to be big enough to house as many as twelve men apiece and be of uniform size and shape—sixteen feet long by fourteen feet wide, with walls six and a half feet high. Each was to have a door at one end, with fireplace and chimney facing it at the other. A firm believer in competition, Washington offered a prize—not of fourteen damsels but of twelve dollars, one dollar for each man—to the unit in each regiment that got its hut finished first.

The building of huts was hampered by various shortages. One, since the British had burned the local sawmill along with other Valley Forge resources, was that of boards for doors and roofing. Another was noted by Colonel Henry B. Livingston in his diary for Christmas Eve: ". . . We . . . are now building huts for our winter quarters without nails or tools so that I suppose we may possibly render ourselves very comfortable by the time winter is over." Actually, there were enough axes, and enough expert woodsmen using them, to make the job a reasonably quick one. The winners of the first twelve-dollar prize had their hut finished by evening of the second day in camp; and by the third of January—though Washington noted

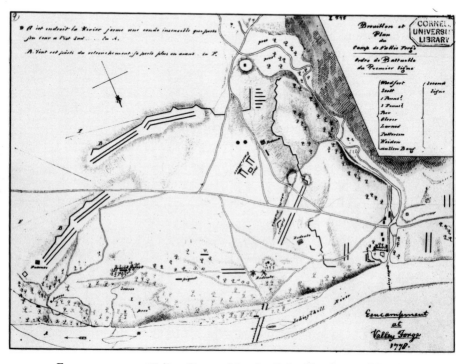

Encampment at Valley Forge. Map by Brigadier General Louis LeBeque du Portail, chief of the French engineers with the Continental Army. Nineteenth-century copy of 1778 original.

even then that some of his men were not yet under cover
—most of the cabins were up and occupied.

Laid out face-to-face along the flank of the hill and on
the bank of the river, the huts were naturally far from
commodious. The roofs—crude cedar, pine, or chestnut
shingles—leaked more or less steadily and scarcely served
to shut in what warmth there was from the fires. Gaps in
the log walls were caulked after a fashion with slivers of
wood and handfuls of clay, but this by no means kept out
all the drafts. The fireplaces, burning green wood and
with inadequate chimneys, tended to smoke; and when
the door was opened, to provide a draft, the heat escaped
with the smoke. In most of the cabins, the floors were a
foot or two below ground level for additional protection
from the weather, but this also served to make them
damp. The only bedding—and often the only furniture
except for rough stools, wall pegs and log seats near the
fires—was straw strewn across the muddy floors; and
some of the cabins lacked even that.

Nonetheless, the soldiers were used to such hardships,
and after a chilly autumn spent largely in tents, brush
lean-tos, or without any shelter at all, many of the men
found their cabins—perhaps actually not too different from
the "Quonset huts" of World War II—satisfactory enough.
One private informed his family, with touching regard for
their peace of mind but seemingly not without conviction,
that the army was living "on the fat of the land." At Morristown the year before, Thomas Paine had been inspired to
write grimly about "the times that try men's souls" and to
call attention eloquently to the shortcomings of the "sun-
shine soldier and the summer patriot." Now, paying an-

A soldier's hut in winter, Valley Forge.

RONALD E. HEATON, NORRISTOWN, PENNSYLVANIA.

other brief visit to the army headquarters, he found the scene a much more cheery one and dashed off a blithe eyewitness description to Benjamin Franklin in Paris:

"I was there when the Army first began to build huts. They appeared to me like a family of beavers; everyone busy; some carrying logs, others mud and the rest fastening them together." In fact, the army might well have been exceptionally snug at Valley Forge if the men had had blankets, clothes, shoes, and, most important of all, enough to eat. Unfortunately, these amenities were constantly scarce and sometimes altogether lacking.

According to the regulations fixed by Congress, daily rations for the Continental Army were a pound and a half of flour or bread, a pound of meat or fish, or three-quarters of a pound of pork, and a gill of whiskey or spirits, with an occasional half pint of peas or beans in place of the flour, and beer or milk in addition to the whiskey. At Valley Forge, on the day of the army's arrival, there had been no fresh meat for two days and none turned up for two days afterward. Foraging parties finally found enough mutton and rum to go around in small quantities on Christmas Day, but shortages amounting to an intermittent famine continued thereafter through the winter. On some days many of the men drew no rations whatsoever and on others they had nothing but flour from which to concoct something euphemistically called "fire cake," made by moistening the flour with water and then grilling it over the hot embers.

The food shortage was partly a matter of transportation and partly of real scarcity. The countryside over which the two armies had foraged through most of the autumn

53

had little left to offer. What there was brought twice as much in Philadelphia as it did in the camp where standard commissary rates were three shillings nine pence a pound for butter, ten shillings a bushel for potatoes, and ten pence a pound for veal. In Philadelphia, which was only partially supplied by sea, fresh veal brought four shillings a pound, potatoes sixteen a bushel, and butter seven a pound. Under these conditions, farmers naturally preferred to sell their produce to the enemy; and to prevent their grain from being bought up at low prices by the army, many refused to thresh it at all. Washington retaliated by stating that all unthreshed grain within seventy miles would be confiscated and paid for merely as straw, but the order had little effect.

Congress had appropriated eight thousand barrels of flour for the army's use during the first part of the winter, but most of this remained in warehouses remote from Valley Forge. Such food supplies as were shipped to the camp, moreover, were subject to severe attrition in getting there. Civilian wagoners not only charged exorbitant wages but did as little as possible to earn them. To save space, they emptied flour barrels into open carts, thus exposing their contents to the weather. To lighten their loads on muddy or icy roads, they poured the brine off salt meat, thus causing it to spoil. Salt herring arrived in such condition that the fish had disintegrated into a sort of paste that "had to be shovelled up en masse."

Supplies of clothing were as scant as those of food. Washington had already offered a prize of a hundred dollars for the best substitute for shingle roofing, which no one came forward to claim. When he put up another, this one of ten dollars, for the best rawhide substitute for shoes, it too went unawarded. Men on guard duty turned out in an assortment of odds and ends collected from their hutmates; an unshod sentry stood on his hat to keep his bare feet off the snow.

Up to a point, discomforts shared by any group, and especially a disciplined one like an army, tend to encourage *esprit de corps* and may even raise rather than lower the common morale. Chronicles of arduous campaigns, from Xenophon's in Persia to Napoleon's in Russia, or even of civilian behavior in bombed cities like London, Berlin, or Tokyo during World War II, make it clear that, fortified by numbers, human resilience has wider limits than would ordinarily be assumed. On first arriving at Valley Forge, a tendency to make light of the numerous difficulties was reflected in sardonic jokes and wisecracks of the sort still typical of American military humor.

At Valley Forge one of the first subjects for satiric comment was naturally Mount Joy—all the more when it became established that Mount Misery lay outside the camp boundaries. A regimental surgeon by the euphonious name of Albigence Waldo* recorded a typical appraisal of army food: describing the beef brought into camp, a soldier remarked that the carcass was so thin that he could see the butcher's breeches buttons through it. An officer noticed a group of soldiers cooking a stone in a kettle and asked them why. "Well," was the straight-faced answer, "they say there's strength in a stone—if you can only get it out." Even the lack of clothes lent itself to grim jokes of the same sort: the official Continental uniform

* See Appendix II.

was buff and blue, and it was observed that at Valley Forge the buff at least was amply displayed.

Nonetheless, while shared hardships may provide material for mirth up to a point, the jokes eventually wear thin and become bitter. A day or two after the army reached its winter quarters, a catchphrase made the rounds of the camp, perhaps originally a gruff reply given to an officer by a private and later repeated by his fellows: "No meat, no soldier." Presently the phrase was amplified to "No meat, no coat, no flour, no soldier," becoming a sort of chant that was varied with desolate accompaniments such as the simulated hooting of owls or cawing of crows. These sounds would start in one hut and be picked up by others along a whole street. Then another street or a group of huts in another part of the campground would take up the noise until the whole camp was in an uproar. Listening in his marquee pitched high on the windy hillside, Washington recognized the noise as the voice of incipient mutiny.

For the complete collapse of the supply system at Valley Forge, there were numerous reasons, many of them going back to the outbreak of hostilities in 1775. At that time, Congress had made a brave start by establishing a Commissary Department for purchasing supplies and a Quartermaster Department for delivering these to the army. As head of the former they had chosen Joseph Trumbull, the able son of Governor Jonathan Trumbull of Connecticut. As quartermaster general, they had selected an even more promising figure, in the person of young

Thomas Mifflin of Philadelphia who, at twenty-eight, had sat with Benjamin Franklin as one of Philadelphia's two representatives in Pennsylvania's colonial legislature, and whom John Adams had characterized as "the heart and soul of the Rebellion." Washington had made Mifflin one of his original aides-de-camp with the rank of brigadier general, a post which he held concurrently with the quartermaster generalship.

In Mifflin's case, this sudden eminence had produced unfortunate results. In the summer of 1777, at a series of staff meetings called by Washington to consider his next move, Mifflin had urged that the army proceed to the defense of Philadelphia while General Nathanael Greene argued that it should stay near New York. When Washington followed Greene's advice, Mifflin apparently drew the inference that he was out of favor with the commander in chief. Not long afterward Washington sent him to Philadelphia to give Congress a report on conditions in the field. Mifflin stayed on in the capital, letting his deputies handle the army's supply service until, in the fall of 1777, he fell ill and left Philadelphia for Reading, where he had just bought a new house. In November, he retired as quartermaster general, after indicating that he would have much preferred a command in the field. Congress then left Washington—by now accustomed to dealing with the deputies—to try to handle the job of quartermaster general for himself.

Compared to Mifflin's, Trumbull's record as head of the Commissary Department was, as long as it lasted, reasonably impressive. Perhaps partly because he was somewhat removed from the army politics at headquarters, Trumbull was one of the few major figures in the Revolution who was

57

never subject to hostile criticism. Another reason may have been that he held the post for only two years, after which he too fell ill and resigned. His death soon after was attributed, in the inscription on his Lebanon, Connecticut, tombstone, to "the perpetual cares and fatigues" of his office.

Prior to Trumbull's resignation as commissary general in August 1777, supplies had been adequately maintained, but under his successor, William Buchanan, perhaps partly due to Trumbull's failure to plan ahead for larger purchases, shortages began to develop. In the summer of 1777, against Washington's advice, Congress tried to remedy the situation by a complex and cumbersome reorganization of the Commissary Department into a Bureau of Supply and a Bureau of Issue. By autumn, this reorganization and resignations due both to it and to the change in chiefs, combined with ordinary difficulties like lack of funds, mismanagement, and graft, had put the Commissary Department in far worse shape than it had been before.

At the end of 1777 the whole creaking machinery slowed down to a virtual standstill, with predictable consequences. As to shoes, uniforms, and blankets, most of the limited stores on hand at Lancaster, Reading, or elsewhere were either not shipped at all or, like the food shipments, often entrusted to dishonest or incompetent wagoners who failed to deliver them. When ordered to turn in their tents for repair and storage until spring, many of the men instead cut them up to use for shirts, breeches, or foot wrappings.

Ample supplies of clothes on order from France and the

French West Indies were held up by various shipping difficulties. Uniforms for the Pennsylvania regiment were not dispatched from nearby warehouses because the Council of the State had neglected to authorize their issue. One shipment of coats that did reach camp was found to be unserviceable because the manufacturer had neglected to sew on the buttons. When Anthony Wayne drew on his considerable private means to the extent of forty-five hundred pounds in an effort to rectify these mishaps, the clothier general refused to authorize the transaction on the grounds that it was "irregular."

According to Du Portail's original plan, officers at the Valley Forge camp were to occupy huts identical with those of the men. In fact, while most colonels and below stuck to this scheme, most of the field-grade officers found some sort of private habitation in the neighborhood of the camp. One French officer, Colonel Buysson, established himself in a cave that a local farmer had remodeled into a springhouse. The quarters chosen for the commander in chief stood close to the main crossroads of the village and belonged to Mrs. Deborah Hewes, whose late husband had owned the village forge. When she requested a few days grace in which to pack up her belongings, the commander in chief considerately postponed moving in for a week. Meanwhile, from the shabby tent which he had used through three campaigns, he outlined the army's situation in detail to Henry Laurens, president of Congress, writing in his own hand on December 23:

"Sir: . . . I am now convinced, beyond a doubt that unless some great and capital change suddenly takes place

. . . this Army must inevitably . . . Starve, dissolve, or disperse, in order to obtain subsistence in the best manner they can. . . .

"Yesterday afternoon receiving information that the Enemy, in force, had left the City, and were advancing towards Derby with apparent design to forage, . . . I or.der'd the Troops to be in readiness, that I might give every opposition in my power; when . . . to my great mortification, I was not only informed, but convinced, that the Men were unable to stir on Acct. of Provision, and that a dangerous Mutiny begun the Night before, and which with difficulty was suppressed was still much to be apprehended . . .

"This brought forth the only [Commissary] in this Camp; and, with him, this Melancholy and alarming truth; that he had not a single hoof of any kind to Slaughter, and not more than 25. Barl. of Flour! From hence form an opinion of our Situation when I add, that, he could not tell when to expect any.

"All I could do under the circumstances was, to send out a few light Parties to watch and harrass the Enemy, whilst other Parties were instantly detached different ways to collect, if possible, as much Provision as would satisfy the present pressing wants of the Soldiery. But will this answer? No Sir: three or four days bad weather would prove our destruction. What then is to become of the Army this Winter? . . . I have been tender heretofore of giving any opinion, or lodging complaints, as the change [in the Quartermaster's Department] took place contrary to my judgment, and the consequences thereof were predicted; yet, finding that the inactivity of the

Army, whether for want of provisions, Cloaths, or other essentials, is charged to my Acct. . . . it is time to speak plain . . . with truth then I can declare that, no Man, in my opinion, ever had his measures more impeded than I have, by every department of the Army.

"Since the Month of July, we have had no assistance from the Quarter Master Genl. and to want of assistance from this department, the Commissary Genl. charges great part to his deficiency; to this I am to add, that notwithstanding it is a standing order (and often repeated) that the Troops shall always have two days Provisions by them, that they may be ready at any sudden call, yet, no opportunity has scarce ever yet happened of taking advantage of the Enemy that has not been either totally obstructed or greatly impeded on this Acct. . . .

"We find Gentlemen [a Congressional investigating group that had visited the camp in the fall] without knowing whether the Army was really going into Winter Quarters or not reprobating the measure as much as if they thought Men [the Soldiery] were made of Stocks or Stones and equally insensible of frost and Snow and moreover, as if they conceived it easily practicable for an inferior Army under the disadvantages I have describ'd our's to be wch. is by no means exaggerated to confine a superior one (in all respects well appointed, and provided for a Winters Campaign) within the City of Phila., and to cover from depredation and waste the States of Pensa., Jersey, &ca. . . . I can assure those Gentlemen that it is a much easier and less distressing thing to draw remonstrances in a comfortable room by a good fire side than to occupy a cold bleak hill and sleep under frost and Snow

61

without Cloaths or Blankets; however, although they seem to have little feeling for the naked, and distressed Soldier, I feel superabundantly for them, and from my Soul pity those miseries, wch. it is neither in my power to relieve or prevent."

As the winter wore on, Washington's problems of providing food, clothing, and shelter not only remained unsolved but became increasingly acute; and to them were added others, primarily of health and discipline. The army at Valley Forge won immortal renown for enduring the hardships of the camp, but what those who stayed had to endure is perhaps shown most clearly by the substantial number who chose instead to go elsewhere.

The claim that the defection of some hundreds of U.S. prisoners of war during the Korean War was unprecedented in U.S. Army annals bears small resemblance to the truth. During the Revolution, in which far fewer troops were involved, desertions ran into the thousands; and while many of the deserters merely went home or rejoined under another name to secure the bounty for enlistment, more than a thousand joined the British at Philadelphia in 1778 alone—not as a result of indoctrination applied under pressure but of their own free will and at considerable personal risk.

According to the tables kept by Philadelphia's able Tory mayor, Joseph Galloway, who was also Howe's intelligence chief, most of the defectors were "old country men," that is, immigrants from Britain or elsewhere who were presumably less firmly committed to the rebel cause than native-born Americans. However, the total also included 283 of the latter, a surprisingly large number only until one recalls that the moral superiority of the rebel cause, which most Americans now take for granted, was at that time thoroughly moot. As in all civil wars, many families had members fighting for both sides; and while Benedict Arnold was the only colonial officer who actually sold out, there were many others, like Charles Lee, whose loyalties obviously wavered. Meanwhile, neutrality was not only a common but a thoroughly respectable position, as illustrated dramatically by the Quaker, James Vaux, at whose commodious house near Valley Forge George Washington himself dined and spent a night in mid-September 1777. What made this visit noteworthy was that Sir William Howe had been Vaux's houseguest the night before, so that the table at which Washington dined was the one at which Howe had had his breakfast the same morning.

While Benedict Arnold has gone down in history as the top traitor of the war, for pure diligence in treason he was far outdistanced by numerous noncommissioned bounty jumpers. Of these the most spectacular was an extraordinary Irish resident of Valley Forge known as Big Jim Fitzpatrick. Newly arrived in Pennsylvania as an indentured blacksmith's assistant, Fitzpatrick, apparently bored by the sobrieties of life in a small Quaker settlement, signed up for the Pennsylvania Militia soon after the hostilities started. His first desertion took place shortly thereafter in New York when he and a friend swam the Hudson River and walked back to Valley Forge where they were soon arrested. Offered freedom from the Walnut Street jail in

Philadelphia on condition that they report back to their regiments, the two instead once more returned to Valley Forge where, the next time he was turned in, Fitzpatrick scared off his would-be captors by threatening to shoot them all with his army rifle.

When Howe arrived in Pennsylvania, Fitzpatrick, who had concluded that he might by now be *persona non grata* to the Colonial Army, joined the British, fought against his former comrades at Brandywine and shortly thereafter found himself once more in Philadelphia. Apparently feeling that his varied military achievements entitled him by now to a higher rank, Fitzpatrick assumed that of captain. This step brought him to the attention of his superiors, who, though they deplored the means of his promotion, were even more impressed by his potential abilities as a spy and forage scout in the surrounding countryside.

The role of spy was one for which Fitzpatrick's relish was as conspicuous as his aptitude, and in it he quickly attained wide renown. Once when a party of fifty armed men set out to capture him and, having failed, were refreshing themselves in a local tavern, Fitzpatrick entered, covered the room with his rifle, called for a drink with which he toasted all present and only departed after ceremoniously smashing the glass. On another occasion, when a troup of twenty men were searching for him, he singled out the leader, promised to escort him to "Fitz," and, having thus decoyed him away from his comrades, tied him to a tree and flogged him with a grapevine. Not until his whereabouts were betrayed by his blacksmith-employer's daughter, with whom he had been conducting an intermittent liaison during spare moments in his lively career as turncoat, was Fitzpatrick finally captured by a Captain Robert McAfee of the Pennsylvania State Militia. Convicted of burglary, treason, and desertion, Fitzpatrick was eventually hanged, while McAfee used his reward of a thousand dollars to open a local tavern.

In dealing with the problem of more commonplace desertions, Washington enjoyed the advantage of living in an age when corporal punishments of a severity later frowned upon were in common use. Originally the penalty for simple desertion was thirty-nine lashes on the bare back—a number long traditional in other armies and apparently derived from Biblical precept (II Cor. 11:24): "Of the Jews, five times received I forty stripes save one." By June 1776, Congress had upped the limit to one hundred and it was soon extended considerably more, though never to the extreme bounds approved in the services of the mother country. (In the British Army, whose lower ranks were largely composed of jailbirds and guttersnipes impressed into the service against their will, sentences of a thousand lashes were reasonably common, while British Navy records include the case of a captain who, when one of his seamen died while being "flogged around the fleet" with fifty lashes of his sentence still uninflicted, ordered them to be administered to the corpse.) However, to make up for such moderation in respect of simple floggings, numerous refinements of various sorts calculated to make chastisement more humiliating or painful were applied, including application to the affected area, as a restorative immediately after a flogging, of a pailful of cold water.

Desertion was by no means the only, or even the most

common, misdeed which the Valley Forge courts-martial were called upon to remedy. The roster included trading with the enemy, embezzling, theft, drunkenness, conduct unbecoming a gentleman, dueling, and gambling. Though Washington himself in peacetime enjoyed betting on the races or a hand at cards, he considered gambling in the army a vice of "so pernicious a nature that it will never escape the severest punishments." Among the penalties imposed for serious offenses was that, in the case of a commissary found guilty of theft, of being "mounted on a horse backforemost without a saddle, his coat turned wrong side out his hands tied behind him & be drum'd out of the Army (Never more to return)." For fraudulently detaining two months' pay from a soldier, a captain was sentenced to be cashiered. A lieutenant "tryed first for Attempting to commit sodomy . . . 2nd for perjury" was found guilty on both counts and sentenced to dismissal with infamy "to be drummed out of Camp tomorrow Mg. by all the Drums and Fifes in the Army never to return."

Most lenient of the penalties prescribed by the commander in chief was naturally that for the peccadillo of drunkenness which, in the case of both officers or privates, consisted of hacking down to ground level one of the hundreds of stumps left from the trees cut for huts and abatis. This led to one of Washington's few moments of relative hilarity at Valley Forge when, riding across the parade ground with his staff, he came upon a private cutting the only stump in the area and stopped for a chat with him:

"Well, my good fellow," said the general, "I see you have found the last stump."

"Yes," was the private's grumbling reply, "and now when an officer gets drunk, there'll be no stump to cut."

According to Washington's adjutant general, Colonel Alexander Scammel, whose function on the staff included that of camp jester, the commander in chief "laughed heartily and some of the officers felt a sensation of great relief."

While the record of the courts-martial held at Valley Forge and the punishments decreed by them may now-adays seem shocking, they no doubt helped to check the abuses they were intended to correct. Even more damaging to the army than desertion and defection, however, were deaths from disease, which during the whole period in winter quarters accounted for some twenty-five hundred men, or twenty-five percent of the force that had arrived in camp at Christmastime. For disease, of course, punishments were of no avail whatsoever—although small comprehension of this fact was suggested by most of the treatments in fashion at the period.

Since medical science in 1778 had not yet detected the close connection between body lice and "camp fever," or typhus, the method customarily used at Valley Forge to prevent the spread of this deservedly dreaded infection consisted of burning a spoonful of sulfur or gunpowder inside the huts every day. The smoke thus produced, per-haps because it gave off an offensive smell, was considered to have noteworthy therapeutic powers. Once typhus had been contracted despite this regimen, it usually took a fatal course impeded little by the recommended treatment of dieting on mutton broth and Madeira.

The main rival to typhus as a killer was smallpox—of

which Washington himself had experienced a severe case at nineteen, when traveling in the West Indies with his brother Lawrence. As to this scourge, doctors had, to be sure, already discovered that serious cases could often be warded off by innoculating the potential patient with a mild attack on purpose. Unhappily, there was much danger and discomfort but little precision in this precaution; and furthermore, although Washington was such a firm believer in inoculation that he had induced his wife to try it in 1776, the shortage of surgeons and serum at Valley Forge was such that months went by before the whole camp population could thus be partially immunized. Meanwhile, the spread of both smallpox and typhus was encouraged by the circumstance that the early symptoms —high fever, rigor, headache, and sleeplessness—were common to both, so that sufferers from one ailment were likely to be treated for the other. Segregation of the two types of patients was, of course, out of the question; and bedding was far too scarce to permit the luxury of a change of straw for each new occupant of a pallet when its previous one died or, in rare instances, recovered.

In view of the high incidence of contagious disease, the hospital facilities at and near Valley Forge were understandably capacious. Biggest of the base hospitals was at Yellow Springs, formerly a health resort for spa-minded Philadelphians. A chain of lesser establishments had also been set up at Bethlehem, Ephrata, Lititz and other accessible communities where the sisters and brothers of numerous resident religious orders helped with the nursing.

At the camp itself, each row of huts had a sick bay of

sorts for use when no other accommodations were available, or in case of minor ailments. The latter included the numerous amputations performed in the camp surgery, without benefit of anesthesia other than that provided by biting a bullet, which were often necessitated by cases of frostbite severe enough to result in gangrene of the hand or foot. However, while hospital space was extensive, it was so far from adequate to the demands made on it that twenty men ordinarily occupied rooms barely big enough for eight.

Prior to the era of modern nursing, inaugurated under somewhat analogous circumstances during the Crimean War by Florence Nightingale, care of the inmates in all army hospitals had always been the province primarily of "camp women." While the three hundred or so wives, sweethearts, and prostitutes who accompanied the rebel soldiers into camp at Valley Forge were pressed into service in this capacity, there were never anything like enough to go around. Sanitation was naturally at a minimum and administration generally so bad that even before Valley Forge Benjamin Rush, Surgeon General of the army's medical department who had resigned after a tiff with Dr. William Shippen, Jr., its Director-General, felt obliged to write a highly indignant pamphlet on the subject. However, while Rush's 1777 treatise entitled *Directions for Preserving the Health of Soldiers* proposed commendably specific improvements, it failed to set forth how these were to be effected in view of the existing shortages of personnel and provisions. Meanwhile, though precise statistics were understandably scarce under the circumstances, the therapeutic value of hospitalization was suggested by the experience of one Virginia regiment in which, out of forty members who were hospitalized, only three survived. Less typical was the fine record of the hospital at Lititz where out of fifteen hundred patients admitted, only five hundred died.

In the context of medical history for the period, the experience of Valley Forge was by no means unusual. In the Seven Years' War a few years before, the British Army's toll was 1512 men lost in action and 134,000 from other causes, and these figures were by no means atypical. Nonetheless, while the health record at Valley Forge was not exceptionally bad, some twenty-five hundred deaths during the winter seriously aggravated the effect of defections and desertions upon Washington's already rapidly diminishing army; and this did not include the number of those incapacitated by illness or injury, some of whom eventually received medical discharges.

Even the soldiers who remained on duty in the camp were by no means immune to health problems of their own. Of these the most discomforting, usually described with terse precision as "the itch," was a form of scabies which when scratched often caused more or less serious infections. Equally prevalent was, of course, the common cold, which often developed into pneumonia and thus, in the absence of antibiotic treatment, increased the toll of fatalities; while poisoning of various sorts, brought on by unsanitary food preservation or preparation, often gave rise to various forms of dysentery. The latter tended to aggravate the basic problem of camp sanitation which became increasingly acute. Soldiers who were ill, in addition to being inadequately clothed for inclement weather, were understandably reluctant to pick their way on bare feet at night through muddy, snowy, or icy camp streets, to the camp "vaults" or latrines. One result was that the air in the huts became so foul that General Anthony Wayne may have been guilty of understatement when he said he would rather go into battle than on an inspection tour. Another was that the sentries of some regiments were ordered to fire on any man seen relieving himself in the company streets.

A final problem in hygiene was provided by the bodies of artillery or baggage train horses which died of starvation and exposure. Removing their carcasses was obviously a task of the first magnitude, but burying them in the frozen ground was even more difficult, and the graves were often shallow. After a heavy rain or thaw, the rotting remains would then be exposed so that the job had to be done a second or third time. Before the winter was over, a total of fifteen hundred horses had died in the camp or near it, and two fatigue parties a week were charged with keeping the carcasses interred. Washington, who has often been criticized for his failure to make better use of cavalry, especially during the first years of the war, was a Virginia connoisseur of horseflesh upon whom the misfortunes of the army's baggage animals made a deep impression. "Could the poor horses tell their tale," he remarked in one letter to Congress, "it would be in a strain still more lamentable than the men's, as numbers have actually died of pure want."

According to the late General Lord Allenby, a well-qualified expert on such matters, the main worry for a commander in chief is rarely his adversary in the field.

This constitutes a straightforward matter which qualified subordinates can usually be counted on to cope with. What a commander in chief, as distinct from his subordinates, has to worry about most are such things as integrating his strategy with national policy; attracting foreign allies and maintaining sound relations with them; and, most essential of all, his own position vis-à-vis his government and his army. Rarely has this view of a commander's concerns been better demonstrated than in the case of Washington at Valley Forge. The sorry condition of the draft animals; the health of the army generally; and such related matters as discipline, shelter, clothing, and food were of course constantly on his mind and needed to be dealt with daily. Underlying all these, however, were even graver problems on the solutions to which depended his ability to deal with the more tangible ones. Most troubling of these graver problems as the winter wore on at Valley Forge was the growing intrigue, in both Congress and the army itself, against him and on behalf of General Gates.

5

MAJOR GENERAL HORATIO GATES, the hero of Saratoga, was a British-trained officer who, having served as a captain under Braddock, returned to England after the French and Indian War ended in 1763. Blocked from advancement in the British army by limited funds and an undistinguished lineage, he had turned for a time to "guzzling and gaming" until, after a religious conversion, he retired to a quiet life in the country. In 1773, he bought a tobacco plantation in Virginia where he was living when hostilities began.

Appointed Adjutant General of the Colonial Army in 1775, Gates had shown sufficient competence in that capacity to be given command of the Northern Army in 1777. At Saratoga, where his adversary was on unfamiliar ground with troops exhausted by their long midsummer trek from Canada, Gates also had a numerical advantage roughly eighteen thousand to seven. Indeed, in view of Burgoyne's deficiencies, the results might well have been much the same no matter who had headed the Colonial Army, of which Benedict Arnold and Daniel Morgan actually had immediate command as the action developed in the field. Nonetheless, Saratoga was undeniably a stunning victory—and as the official victor Gates was clearly entitled to much of the credit. What was more open to question was his manner of accepting it.

For Gates, the most appropriate means of announcing his success would have been simply to send a messenger to his commander in chief. Instead—as though he were Washington's equal in rank and held an entirely independent command—he chose to send one directly to Congress. While a case could have been made for that procedure, in view of the importance of the news, it might still have aroused Washington's curiosity, if not his resentment. On the contrary, having gotten news of the victory indirectly from General Israel Putnam on October 17, he waited two weeks more for word from Gates. Failing to get it even then, he wrote his subordinate a letter in which the unavoidable mention of Gates's rudeness was so tactful as to add rather than detract from the warmth of his congratulations:

> Head Quarters near White Marsh
> 15 Miles from Philadelphia, October 30, 1777

Sir: By this Opportunity, I do myself the pleasure to congratulate you on the signal success of the Army under your command, in compelling Genl. Burgoyne and his whole force, to surrender themselves prisoners of War. An Event that does the highest honor to the American Arms, and which, I hope, will be attended with the most extensive and happy consequences. At the same time, I cannot but regret, that a matter of such magnitude and so interesting to our General Operations, should have reached me by report only, or thro' the Channel of Letters, not bearing that authenticity, which the importance of it required, and which it would have received by a line under your signature, stating the simple fact.

The letter was conveyed to Gates in Albany by Alexander Hamilton whose mission also included requesting some reinforcements from the now less urgently active Northern Army.

Making Congress rather than Washington the sole di-

Major General Horatio Gates, commander of the Northern Army in 1777.

rect recipient of his report was by no means Gates's only mistake in announcing his victory. A second, and as it turned out, even more serious one lay in his choice of a messenger. This was a twenty-one-year-old lieutenant colonel named James Wilkinson who took so long to make the 285-mile ride from Albany to York that, when Congress later rewarded him with a commission as a brigadier general, one member remarked that a more appropriate token of its esteem might well have been a pair of spurs. Among Wilkinson's numerous pauses on his sixteen-day jaunt, the least judicious of all was the last before reaching York, at Reading. Here he ran into General Lord Stirling who, recovering from a riding accident and eager for gossip and good company, invited him to stay on for "a pot-luck supper."

An American ironmaster whose inheritance of a British earldom had been disallowed chiefly because the vast land grant which went with it, comprising Nova Scotia, New Brunswick, and most of Maine as well as Nantucket, Martha's Vineyard, and parts of Long Island seemed far too extensive to be handed over to a mere colonial, Stirling, who chose to use the title anyway, also had other claims to renown. One of these was an addiction to strong drink so famous as to have been portrayed in a British farce in New York during the British occupation. In that, the colonial nobleman was shown demanding refreshment from an unruly servitor who replied: "You drank enough stinkabus last night to split the head of an Indian."

Whether, on the occasion of his encounter with Wilkinson, the American earl justified his reputation for conviviality remains a question. Wilkinson, in any case, perhaps encouraged by the nature of the competition, clearly exceeded his own more limited capacities so far as to render him unable thereafter to provide a coherent account of the evening's conversation. Such an account was, however, conveyed to the earl the next morning by one of his own aides, and Stirling lost no time in passing the gist of it along to his commander in chief. In a long report to Valley Forge dealing with routine matters, he inked in a postscript to the effect that one of young Wilkinson's items of gossip was that Gates had recently received a letter from General Thomas Conway saying, among other things, that "Heaven has been determined to save your country or a weak General and bad counselors would have ruined it."

In the extraordinary roster of European military adventurers attracted by the Revolution, Conway was colorful enough to deserve a special niche. An Irish-born Frenchman with wide experience as an officer in the French Army, he had, like many others, been recruited in Paris and commissioned a brigadier general. Since then he had contrived to incur the intense dislike of most of his fellow officers, in part because of his persistent habit of asking them such questions as: "Did Congress see you before they appointed you?" Among those to whom he had endeared himself least was the commander in chief who was further irritated by Conway's efforts to get Congress to promote him to a major generalcy over the heads of colonial brigadiers whose services he needed more and who, if Conway succeeded, might well resent it to the point of resigning their commissions. Now, given this favorable

chance to enlighten Conway as to his standing at headquarters and at least one of the reasons for it, Washington
wrote to him as follows:

"Sir: a letter which I receivd last night containd the
following paragraph: 'In a letter from Genl. Conway to
Genl. Gates, he says: "Heaven has been determind to
save your country; or a weak General and bad councellors
would have ruind it.' I am Sir Yr. Hble Servt., G. Washington."

This terse note to Conway served to initiate a series of
further missives which were soon shuttling back and forth
between York, Albany, and Valley Forge in a profusion
that must have bewildered even the participants. First
item in the series was a letter from Conway's crony,
Thomas Mifflin, informing Gates that an extract from
Conway's letter to him had somehow been relayed to
Washington. Gates's response to this was to dash off three
highly agitated letters of his own. One was to Conway,
asking him which of his letters had been "copied" and
requesting his aid in discovering who had done the copy-
ing. Another was to Mifflin, requesting his assistance to
the same end. The third was to Washington saying that he
was horrified by the discovery that Conway's confidential
"letters" to him had apparently been read by some unau-
thorized outsider, implying that the guilty party might
have been Alexander Hamilton during his visit a few
weeks before; and asking Washington to help track down
the culprit. To compound the other errors in this naïve
screed, Gates informed Washington that, in the interests
of national security, he was also sending a copy of it to the
president of Congress.

Gates's decision to send a copy of his letter to Congress provided Washington with an opportunity which he speedily and effectively utilized in his reply, dispatched from Valley Forge on the fourth of January:

Sir: Your letter of the 8th, Ulto. came to my hands a few days ago; and, to my great surprize informed me, that a Copy of it had been sent to Congress, for what reason, I find myself unable to acct.; but, as some end doubtless was intended to be answered by it, I am laid under the disagreeable necessity of returning my answer through the same channel, lest any Member of that Honble. body, should harbour an unfavourable suspicion of my having practiced some indirect means, to come at the contents of the confidential Letters between you and General Conway.

I am to inform you then, that Colo. Wilkenson, in his way to Congress in the Month of Octobr. last, fell in with Lord Stirling at Reading, and, not in confidence that I ever understood, inform'd his Aid de Camp Majr. McWilliams that General Conway had written thus to you,

Heaven has been determined to save your Country; or a weak General and bad Counsellors* would have ruined it.

[Washington put an asterisk beside "Counsellors" and wrote at the bottom of the page: "One of whom, by the by, he was."]

Lord Stirling from motives of friendship, transmitted the acct. with this remark.

The inclosed was communicated by Colonl. Wilkinson to Majr. McWilliams, such wicked duplicity of conduct I shall always think it my duty to detect.

79

In consequence of this information, and without having any thing more in view than merely to shew that Gentn. that I was not unapprized of his intrieguing disposition, I wrote him a Letter in these Words.

Sir. A Letter which I received last night contained the following paragraph.

In a Letter from Genl. Conway to Genl. Gates he says, "Heaven has been determined to save your Country; or a weak General and bad Counsellors would have ruined it."

I am Sir &ca.

Neither this Letter, nor the information which occasioned it, was ever, directly, or indirectly communicated by me to a single Officer in this Army (out of my own family) excepting the Marquis de la Fayette, who, having been spoken to on the Subject by Genl. Conway, applied for, and saw, under injunctions of secrecy, the Letter which contained Wilkenson's information; so desirous was I, of concealing every matter that could, in its consequences, give the smallest Interruption to the tranquility of this Army, or afford a gleam of hope to the enemy by dissentions therein.

Thus Sir, with an openess and candour which I hope will ever characterize and mark my conduct have I complied with your request; the only concern I feel upon the occasion (finding how matters stand) is, that in doing this, I have necessarily been obliged to name a Gentn. whom I am perswaded (although I never exchanged a word with him upon the Subject) thought he was rather doing an act of Justice, than committing an act of infidility; and sure I am, that, till Lord Stirling's Letter came to my hands, I never knew that General Conway (who I viewed in the light of a stranger to you) was a corrispondant of yours, much less did I suspect that I was the subject of your confidential Letters; pardon me then for adding, that so far from conceiving that the safety of the States can be affected, or in the smallest degree injured, by a discovery of this kind, or, that I should be called upon in such solemn terms to point out the author, that I considered the information as coming from yourself; and given with a friendly view to forewarn, and consequently forearm me, against a secret enemy; or, in other words, a dangerous incendiary; in which character, sooner or later, this Country will know Genl. Conway. But, in this, as in other matters of late, I have found myself mistaken. I am, etc.

On learning for the first time that his own trusted aide had been, via Lord Stirling, Washington's informant, Gates replied in a voluminous tract which offered a somewhat blurred apology, castigated Wilkinson, praised Conway, and denied the accuracy of the Stirling quotation. Washington's response to this was even more caustic than his reply to its predecessor. In it he remarked that he found "no small difficulty in reconciling the spirit and import of your different Letters, and sometimes of different parts of the same Letter with each other." He pointed out that Gates's obvious reluctance to make public the contents of Conway's letter implied that, if it did not contain precisely the words quoted by Stirling, it might contain even worse. Finally, he dealt with Conway:

"It is however greatly to be lamented, that this adept in Military science did not employ his abilities in the progress of the Campaign, in pointing out those wise measures, which were calculated to give us 'that degree of success we might reasonably expect.' The United States have lost much from that unseasonable diffidence, which prevented his embracing the numerous opportunities he had in Council, of displaying those rich treasures of knowledge and experience he has since so freely laid open to you. . . ."

What Conway's original letter to Gates actually said was never revealed, although Henry Laurens, who did see a copy, later recalled that, while it did not contain the paragraph Wilkinson had quoted, it contained "ten times worse," including the line, "What a pity there is but one Gates."

If Conway's detractions had been the only ones he had to deal with, Washington's concern might have seemed somewhat excessive. Unfortunately, he had considerably more. Early in January, his loyal friend Patrick Henry had forwarded him a long anonymous letter arguing that Gates's victory at Saratoga showed what a good general could do and suggesting that under his command the troops at Valley Forge might be capable of simliar prodigies.

"I am sorry," said Governor Henry in his covering note, "that there should be one man who counts himself my friend who is not yours." From President Laurens came a somewhat similar document called "Thoughts of a Freeman" which had been handed to him by someone on the stairs of the building in York where Congress held its sessions. The substance of the latter and the calligraphy of the former suggested that Dr. Benjamin Rush had had some hand in the composition of both. What made this particularly troubling was, as Washington noted in thanking Patrick Henry, that Dr. Rush "has been elaborate and studied in his professions of regard for me, and long since the letter to you." Nonetheless, if the obviously growing opposition to him, which was clearly shared by some who pretended to be his loyal friends, had been expressed only in epistolary terms, the commander in chief might still have felt reasonably secure. What made his footing so dangerous was that other and even more tangible signs of hostility within Congress and elsewhere were becoming increasingly evident. The most alarming of these concerned an organization called the Board of War and the matter of appointing an inspector general of the army.

That Washington had lost the close battles of Brandywine and Germantown, and thus the colonial capital, was due to several factors, among which perhaps the most important, and certainly the most remediable, was his army's incompetence in the most basic rudiments of maneuver. According to legend, the colonies won the Revolution largely because of their army's superior skill in firing from behind tree trunks at clumsy Redcoats lined up in solid ranks in the open. Actually, they almost lost it because of the army's inability to march except in ragged single files which presented a long exposed flank and caused fatal delays in forming a compact line of fire. Forced now into a season of inactivity, Washington had resolved to employ the time in correcting the faults to which he largely owed his sorry situation. The question now was how best to go about it.

When confronted with a problem of this sort, Washington's first impulse was usually to call for a staff meeting.

83

The outcome on this occasion, endorsed by five major generals and ten brigadiers, was that a special agency on Washington's staff be charged with improving discipline and training. The head of this new staff department, to be known as the inspector general, would be responsible for preparing a whole new system of drill regulations which, instead of varying from regiment to regiment like the existing ones, would be made uniform throughout the whole army. Assistant inspectors in the various brigades and divisions would then help the inspector general to train the troops to execute them. When Washington thereupon wrote to President Laurens, recommending the immediate establishment of the inspector generalship, Congress referred the choice of an officer to fill the post to the then newly reorganized Board of War.

Like the inspector generalship itself, the Board of War was an organization which, when first proposed, enjoyed the full approval of the commander in chief. Its function —analogous to that now fulfilled by the Department of Defense—was simply to serve as a liaison with Congress in military matters which that body as a whole lacked both the time and the expertise to handle. Since the object was to achieve full cooperation in running the war between the top command and a group of Congressional specialists, at least some members of the board would also be members of the commander in chief's immediate "family." However, lest the board become too subservient to the commander, Congress had included a proviso in its organization chart that made its proceedings subject to regular fortnightly inspections by Congress and open at all times to inspection by any individual delegate.

When Congress undertook to reorganize the Board of War in the fall of 1777, any possibility of subservience to the commander in chief was even more effectively precluded. It developed then that on the new board only one member of the commander's staff was to be included, in the person of Colonel Timothy Pickering, Gates's successor as adjutant general, who could rarely be spared from headquarters to attend its meetings. The other four were Richard Peters, who, as secretary of the previous board, was familiar with its past proceedings; Joseph Trumbull, as an expert in commissary matters; Thomas Mifflin, the former quartermaster general; and General Horatio Gates himself. Gates, indeed, would be the board's president, and "officiate at the Board, or in the field, as occasion may require."

That of the four active members of the new board the two most influential were leaders of the anti-Washington faction may well have struck the commander in chief as a doubtful augury for its future activities. If so, his forebodings were speedily confirmed when, on December 10, the board recommended a plan for the inspector generalship concocted by none other than the redoubtable General Conway. According to this scheme, the inspector general would not only have the already broad powers recommended by Washington. He would in addition function quite independently of the commander in chief and report directly to the board. Three days later, Congress adopted this plan.

Making the inspector general independent of the commanding general established what Chief Justice John Marshall, then a lieutenant at Valley Forge, was later in

85

his five-volume life of Washington, learnedly to describe as "an *imperium in imperio*." Enabling him to report directly to a board already heavily prejudiced against the commander in chief made it clear that this *imperium in imperio* would be used against the latter. The Congress might well have been content to stop at that point but instead it went considerably further. For the post of inspector general, the personage it selected on December 13 was none other than Conway himself; and, ostensibly to make sure that he would have ample rank for the assignment, the board simultaneously gave him the promotion, for which he had been lobbying so busily ever since his arrival, to major general.

In subjecting a post that had been carefully defined by Washington himself, first to redefinition, and then to occupancy by the one general in the army of whom he had expressed outspoken distrust, Congress obviously meant to humiliate the commander in chief. By promoting Conway to a major generalcy, however, Congress had done even more than that. Two months before, on October 17, Washington had written his old friend and neighbor, Virginian delegate Richard Henry Lee, that if there was any truth in a report he had received "that Congress hath appointed, or, as others say, are about to appoint, Brigadier Conway a Major General in this Army, it will be as unfortunate a measure as ever was adopted. I may add (and I think with truth) that it will give a fatal blow to the existence of the Army."

This was explicit enough but the commander in chief went considerably further: ". . . No day passes over my head without application for leave to resign; within the last six days, I am certain, twenty Commissions, *at least*, have been tendered to me. I must therefore, conjure you, to conjure Congress to consider this matter well, and not by a real Act of injustice, compel some good Officers to leave the service, and thereby incur a train of evils unforeseen and irremidiable.

"To Sum up the whole, I have been a Slave to the service: I have undergone more than most Men are aware of, to harmonize so many discordant parts; but it will be impossible for me to be of any further service, if such insuperable difficulties are thrown in my way."

Lee had replied: "No such appointment has been made, nor do I believe it will . . . whilst it is likely to produce the evil consequences you suggest." Lee was proved to have been deceived—or possibly, like Dr. Rush, deceiving. More important than that, the meaningful last sentence of Washington's letter had amounted to a statement that he would hand in his own resignation if Congress promoted Conway over his protest. Now, after two more months in which to think the matter over, Congress had done precisely that.

When Conway arrived in Valley Forge a few days later to take over his new duties, his welcome both from his former colleagues and from the commander in chief was no warmer than might have been expected. Conway departed on December 31 after writing Washington a letter in which not even the bewilderingly eccentric capitalization conceals the astonishing impudence:

What you are pleased to call an extraordinary promotion is a very plain one. there is nothing extraordinary in it, only

Major General Thomas Conway.
ENGRAVING REPRODUCED IN JAMES BENNETT NOLAN'S "GEORGE WASHINGTON
AND THE TOWN OF READING IN PENNSYLVANIA."

that such a place was not thought of Sooner. the General and universal merit, Which you Wish every promoted officer might be endowed with, is a rare gift. We see but few men of merit so generally acknowledged. We know But the great frederick in europe, and the great Washington in this continent. I certainly never was so rash as to pretend to such a prodigious height, neither Do I pretend to any superiority in personal qualities over my Brother Brigadiers for Whom I have much regard, but you, sir, and the great frederick know perfectly well, that this trade is not Learn'd in a few Months. I have served steadily thirty years, that is, before some of my comrades Brigadiers Were Born. therefore I Do not think that it will be found Marvellous and incredible, if I command here a number of men Which falls much short of What I have commanded those many years in an old army.

however, sir, By the complexion of your Letter, and by the two receptions you have honour'd me with since my arrival, I perceive that I have not the happiness of being agreeable to your excellency, and that I can expect no support in fulfilling the Laborious Duty of an inspector general I Do not mean to give you or any officer in the army the Least uneasiness therefore I am very readdy to return to france and to the army where I hope I will Meet with no frowns. I begg Leave to Wish your Excellency a happy New year and a Glorious Campaign.

Back in the circle of his friends at York, Conway complained further of his cool reception, and his complaints reached Washington through the president of Congress to whom he replied on January 2:

Sir: I take the liberty of transmitting you the Inclosed Copies of a Letter, from me to Genl. Conway, since his return from York to Camp, and Two Letters from him to me, which you will be pleased to lay before Congress. I shall not in this Letter animadvert upon them, but after making a single observation submit the whole to Congress.

If General Conway means, by cool receptions . . . that I did not receive him in the language of a warm and cordial Friend, I readily confess the charge. I did not, nor shall I ever, till I am capable of the arts of dissimulation. These I despise, and my feelings will not permit me to make professions of friendship to the man I deem my Enemy, and whose system of conduct forbids it. At the same time, Truth, authorizes me to say, that he was received and treated with proper respect to his Official character, and that he has had no cause to justify the assertion, that he could not expect any support for fulfilling the duties of his Appointment. I have the honor, etc.

In the weeks that followed, the conflict between Conway and the commander in chief about the inspector generalship and the exchange of letters between the commander in chief and Gates about Conway's correspondence with the latter both became matters of public knowledge through Congressional discussion. Early in January, Washington got a letter from his old friend, Dr. James Craik, a Scottish surgeon who had campaigned with him in 1754 and who remained his personal physician until his death, warning him against his enemies in Congress:

Base and Villainous men thro Chagrin, Envy, or Ambition are endeavoring to lessen you in the minds of the people and taking underhanded methods to traduce your Character—

The morning I left Camp I was informed by a Gentleman, whom I believe to be a true Freind of yours, that a strong Faction was forming Against you with the New board of War and in the Congress. it alarmed me exceedingly.

How far Craik's alarm was from groundless was perhaps best indicated fifty years later by John Jay, the delegate from New York who told his son that, since the debates in Congress were not transcribed, the world would never know how strong its opposition to Washington had been. Legend says that the anti-Washington faction in Congress was at one time within a single vote of passing a motion to have the commander in chief arrested and brought to York to stand trial on various charges. This was no doubt an overstatement, but that Washington sensed its deep hostility and knew how he meant to deal with it was shown in his note of thanks to President Laurens for sending him "Thoughts of a Freeman":

"My enemies take an ungenerous advantage of me. They know I cannot combat their insinuations, however injurious, without disclosing secrets, it is of the utmost moment to conceal. But why should I expect to be exempt from censure: the unfailing lot of an elevated situation?"

Late in January, the commander in chief wrote an even more specific statement of his position to an old family friend, the Reverend William Gordon, who was compiling a day-to-day history of the war and who had asked whether there was any truth in the rumor that Washington was about to resign and be replaced:

. . . I am told a scheme of that kind is now on foot by some, in behalf of another gentleman, but whether true or false, whether serious or merely to try the pulse, I neither know nor care; neither interested nor ambitious views led me into the service, I did not solicit the command, but accepted it after much entreaty, with all that diffidence which a conscious want of ability and experience equal to the discharge of so important a trust, must naturally create in a mind not quite devoid of thought; and after I did engage, pursued the great line of my duty, and the object in view (as far as my judgement could direct) as pointedly as the needle to the pole. So soon then as the public gets dissatisfied with my services, or a person is found better qualified to answer her expectation, I shall quit the helm with as much satisfaction, and retire to a private station with as much content, as ever the wearied pilgrim felt upon his safe arrival in the Holyland, or haven of hope; and shall wish most devoutly, that those who come after may meet with more prosperous gales than I have done, and less difficulty. If the expectation of the public has not been answered by my endeavors, I have more reasons than one to regret it; but at present shall only add, that a day may come when the public cause is no longer to be benefited by a concealment of our circumstances; and till that period arrives, I shall not be among the first to disclose such truths as may injure it.

Before this letter reached him, Gordon questioned Washington on the same subject again, and on February 15, Washington dealt with it once more, this time in his own hand and even more clearly:

Dear Sir: Since my last to you abt. the end of Jany. I have been favour'd with your Letter of the 12th. of that Month, which did not reach my hands 'till within these few days. The question there put was, in some degree, solved in my last. But to be more explicit, I can assure you that no person ever heard me drop an expression that had a tendency to resignation, the same principles that led me to imbark in the opposition to the Arbitrary Claims of Great Britain operate with additional force at this day; nor is it my desire to withdraw my Services while they are considered of importance in the present contest; but to report a design of this kind, is among the Arts wch those who are endeavouring to effect a change, are practising, to bring it to pass. I have said, and I still do say, that there is not an Officer in the Service of the United States that would return to the sweets of domestic life with more heart felt joy than I should; but I would have this declaration, accompanied by these Sentiments, that while the public are satisfied with my endeavours I mean not to shrink in the cause; but, the moment her voice, not that of faction, calls upon me to resign, I shall do it with as much pleasure as ever the weary traveller retired to rest. . . .

On hand to celebrate the commander in chief's forty-sixth birthday—which, according to the Gregorian calendar adopted by all the colonies in 1752, fell on Sunday, February 22—was Martha Washington, who had arrived from Mount Vernon a few days before. At forty-five, she was a plump, good-humored woman, not especially pretty or clever, but lively, industrious, and devoted to her son, Jackie Custis, as she had been to her daughter, Patsy, whose sudden death of epilepsy in 1773 had been a crushing blow. Having shared winter quarters with the commander in chief at Cambridge during the first year of the war and at Morristown during the second, she was by now to some

93

degree at home in such establishments. Her impressions of Valley Forge, expressed in a letter to Mercy Warren, the wife of the Massachusetts governor, whom she had met at Cambridge in 1776, were by no means wholly unfavorable.

"The General is in camp, in what is called the great valley on the Banks of the Schuylkill. Officers and men are chiefly in Hutts, which they say is tolerable comfortable; the army are healthy as can well be expected in general.

"The General's apartment is very small; he has had a log Cabin built to dine in, which has made our quarters much more tolerable than they were at first."

Some sixty-eight years later, an old lady of the neighborhood gave the historian, Benson J. Lossing, a picture of the Valley Forge activities of the commander in chief's wife, to whom she referred by a title commonly used at the time:

"I never in my life knew a woman so busy from early morning until late at night as was Lady Washington, providing comforts for the sick soldiers. Every day, excepting Sunday, the wives of officers in camp, and sometimes other women, were invited to Mr. Pott's to assist her in knitting socks, patching garments, and making shirts for the poor soldiers, when materials could be procured. Every fair day she might be seen, with basket in hand, and with a single attendant, going among the huts seeking the keenest and most needy sufferer, and giving all the comforts to them in her power. I sometimes went with her, for I was a stout girl, sixteen years old. On one occasion she went to the hut of a dying sergeant, whose young wife was with him. His case seemed to particularly touch the heart of the good lady, and after she had given him

Washington's headquarters at Valley Forge.

RONALD E. HEATON, NORRISTOWN, PENNSYLVANIA.

some wholesome food she had prepared with her own hands, she knelt down by his straw pallet and prayed earnestly for him and his wife with her sweet and solemn voice. I shall never forget the scene."

When not engaged in errands of mercy, Lady Washington did her best, with some success, to brighten up the social life at headquarters. By the time she arrived in early February, the wives of several other generals were also in the camp. These included Mrs. John Knox, plump and erudite like her husband, and equally affable and jolly; Mrs. Nathanael Greene, who had learned French at her Rhode Island school and with whom once, years later at a Rhode Island ball, Washington danced for three hours in a row; and Lady Stirling with her pretty daughter, Kitty. The ladies normally spent the morning knitting socks and rolling bandages for the soldiers in an upstairs room of the Hewes house where the daily routine was otherwise unpretentious but reasonably comfortable. Dinner took place at three every afternoon, when it was still light enough to obviate need for candles, and often in two shifts until, at Martha Washington's suggestion, the "log Cabin built to dine in" was put up. The company consisted as a rule of the officers who happened to be the major general and the brigadier general of the day; two lieutenant colonels and a brigadier major selected in rotation; the commander in chief's nine aides; and himself. A toast was usually drunk, in rum or whiskey toddy, "to the health of the nation," after which the group sat down to a simple menu of whatever meat was available, frozen potatoes, and bread baked in a house nearby by the camp baker—a redoubtable character named Christopher Ludwig who, previous to his army service, had been a smart Philadelphia caterer whose specialty was gingerbread. Dessert was usually no more than a bowl of hickory nuts which Washington liked to crack with his bare hands.

Aside from Martha's presence in the camp, there was little to distinguish the twenty-second of February, 1778, from the dismal days that had preceded it. Password was Orkney. Countersigns were Ormond and Otway. General orders specified that "The Commissary General is, if possible, to keep the camp well supplied with rice for the use of the sick; if rice cannot be had, Indian meal is to be provided in its place; and as this is an article that can at all times and under all circumstances be had no excuse will be admitted for the neglect." Further along came the customary news from the courts-martial: "Thomas Lawler of the 4th Pennsylvania Regt. tried for deserting to the enemy the 5th of October last, found guilty and sentenced to receive one hundred lashes on his bare back, well laid on. . . ."

Earlier that same week, the commissary had broken down completely for the third time since Christmas, reducing the camp from sparse rations to real famine. At night the crow calls and the owl hoots rose again along the dark hillside, along with the familiar menacing chants: "No pay, no clothes, no provisions, no rum." General Johann de Kalb wrote to a friend in France: "How sad that troops of such excellence, and so much zeal should be so little spared. . . ." And Nathanael Greene wrote to his good friend, Henry Knox, absent for a few days on leave: "Such patience and moderation as they manifested under their sufferings does the highest honor to the magnanimity of the American soldiers. The seventh day (without rations) they came before their superior officers and told their sufferings in as respectful terms as if they had been humble petitioners for special favors; they added that it would be impossible to continue in camp any longer without support." On the sixteenth, the commander in chief had written to Governor George Clinton of New York:

"It is with great reluctance, I trouble you on a subject, which does not properly fall within your province; but it is a subject that occasions me more distress, than I have felt, since the commencement of the war; and which loudly demands the most zealous exertions of every person of weight and authority, who is interested in the success of our affairs. I mean the present dreadful situation of the army for want of provisions, and the miserable prospects before us, with respect to futurity. It is more alarming than you will probably conceive, for, to form a just idea, it were necessary to be on the spot. For some days past, there has been little less, than a famine in camp. A part of the army has been a week, without any kind of flesh, and the rest three or four days. Naked and starving as they are, we cannot enough admire the incomparable patience and fidelity of the soldiery, that they have not been ere this excited by their sufferings, to a general mutiny and dispersion. Strong symptoms, however, of discontent have appeared in particular instances; and nothing but the most active efforts everywhere can long avert so shocking a catastrophe."

Had Washington known of another occurrence that took place on his birthday, he would have been even more concerned. There was a mishap a few miles east of the camp in an area that was being patrolled by an unlucky brigadier named John Lacey. Arriving there on his way back from a foraging expedition with 150 head of fine fat cattle which he had rounded up in southern New Jersey, Major General Anthony Wayne ordered the soldier-drover in charge of them to request an armed escort for the last few miles into camp. Lacey, who had only fifty men in his command and considered the road entirely safe, refused to provide it. The drover went on unescorted and got within eleven miles of the Valley Forge pickets when a force of British dragoons disguised as farmers intercepted his unguarded herd and drove it down the road into Philadelphia.

News of this incident, perhaps fortunately, did not reach headquarters until two days later, and on the twenty-second supper went off much as usual. After the frugal meal, Washington retired to his quarters and the day ended as usual with one small exception. Early that evening the fife and drum corps of a Philadelphia regiment—Proctor's Fourth Continental Artillery Band—paraded down the Gulph Road from the hilltop to the east and played for some time outside headquarters. The commander in chief did not come out to acknowledge the honor, but Martha Washington emerged to thank the bandsmen on his behalf and give them a fifteen-shilling tip. Thus, on what was perhaps the darkest day of the winter and even perhaps of the whole war, Washington's birthday received its first public recognition.

6

ACCORDING TO WIDELY circulated legend, later to be endorsed by the United States Post Office Department in the issuance of a famous commemorative stamp, Washington at Valley Forge was overheard addressing a prayer to the "Ruler of the Universe" while kneeling in the snow in a patch of woods near his headquarters. Like the cherry tree story, the story of the outdoor prayer is based on flimsy evidence, consisting in this case solely of a belated report by the son of the alleged eavesdropper. Nonetheless, whether Washington prayed in the snow or not, he was certainly in sore need of guidance, divine or mundane, and it would have been entirely in keeping with his character to have put in a requisition for it. If he prayed at all, the evening of his birthday would clearly have been the most appropriate time; and for those who believe in the prompt efficacy of such procedures, circumstantial evidence that he did so may be found not only in his reluctance to come down and listen to the band music, but also in at least two events that befell the next day.

One was the arrival of a communication from General Gates in answer to Washington's letter of February 9, which had apparently reached Gates at York on the eighteenth. While Gates's reply did not put a full stop to "the Conway Cabal," it ended the participation of its star protagonist and constituted the closest thing to a sincere and forthright apology that the commander in chief could reasonably have expected from that loquacious correspondent. Gates wrote as follows:

. . . [I] earnestly hope no more of that time, so precious to the public, may be lost upon the subject of General Conway's letter. Whether that gentleman does or does not deserve the suspicions you express, would be entirely indifferent to me, did he not possess an office of high rank in the Army of the United States; for that reason solely I wish he may answer all the expectations of Congress. As to the gentleman, I have no personal connection with him, nor have I any correspondence, previous to his writing the letter which has given offence; nor have I since written to him, save to certify what I know to be the contents of the letter. He therefore must be responsible; as I heartily dislike controversy, even upon my own account, and much more in a matter in which I was only accidentally concerned. In regard to the parts of your Excellency's letter addressed particularly to me, I solemnly declare that I am of no faction; and if any of my letters taken aggregately or by paragraphs convey any meaning, which in any construction is offensive to your Excellency, that was by no means the intention of the writer. After this, I cannot believe your Excellency will either suffer your suspicions or the prejudices of others to induce you to spend another moment upon this subject.

No less generous at the end of the commotion than he had been at the start of it, Washington replied in kind:

I am as averse to controversy, as any Man and had I not been forced into it, you never would have had occasion to impute to me, even the shadow of a disposition towards it. Your repeatedly and Solemnly disclaiming any offensive views, in those matters that have been the subject of our past correspondence, makes me willing to close with the desire, you express, of burying them hereafter in silence, and, as far as future events will permit, oblivion. My temper leads me to peace and harmony with all Men; and it is peculiarly my wish, to avoid any personal feuds with those, who are embarked in the same great National interest with myself, as every difference of this kind must in its consequences be very injurious.

While Gates's earlier blunder in bringing the whole correspondence to the attention of Congress made it impossible, as Washington implied, to consign the dispute to oblivion, the commander in chief's sincerity in offering to do so was amply confirmed by his actions. Not only did he retain Gates as a major commander for the next two years, but later on helped restore his reputation when Gates was under fire for losing the Battle of Camden.

Washington's reply to Gates, dated February 24, might have been even more prompt but for another event that took up most of his attention on February 23. This was the arrival in camp, almost simultaneously with Gates's letter, of a soldier known to U.S. history as Lieutenant General Baron Wilhelm von Steuben. However, while at least the military prefix to this sonorous name and title was largely fictitious, the bearer's abilities soon proved to be as genuine as his arrival at Valley Forge was opportune. Accompanied by a secretary-interpreter, a *valet de chambre*, a private chef, and a handsome Italian greyhound named Azor, the newcomer had reached Valley Forge by a circuitous detour in his military career, starting some fifteen years earlier at the court of the European monarch with' whom Conway had not long before so sarcastically compared his commander in chief.

Baron von Steuben, to give him the benefit of only the nomenclatural embellishments by which he was generally known in Europe, was the grandson of a presumably devout but by no means affluent Hessian parson named Augustine Şteube who, for reasons of his own, had inserted the prestigious "von" before his patronymic and bequeathed it to all his children, including his fourth son who, doubtless assisted thereby, in due course became an officer in the Prussian Army. The grandson of the preacher followed his father's martial footsteps and did so well, especially in the Battle of Rossbach, that by the time he was thirty-three at the end of the Seven Years' War in 1763, he was one of the youngest aides-de-camp to Frederick the Great and a staff officer seemingly in line for a high post in Europe's best army under its greatest captain. At this moment in his career, some mishap, which may possibly have been the discovery of his true family background, resulted in young Von Steuben's sudden and complete fall from favor. He got a job as court chamberlain to the minor royal family of Hohenzollern-Hechingen, in which capacity he spent the next fourteen years and acquired his title of *freiherr*, or baron. When his princely patron encountered financial straits that made it seem appropriate for his court chamberlain to find a less precarious berth elsewhere, Von Steuben in 1777 set off for Paris to look up his old comrade in arms, the Comte de St. Germain, who had just become war minister of France.

Under normal circumstances, the French minister of war might well have been less pleased than embarrassed to reencounter an old friend in urgent need of employment but just now the reverse was the case. Much annoyed at being ejected from North America by the British a few years before, the French were proportionately delighted when the British colonies, no longer dependent on the mother country for defense against their French rivals in Canada, started fighting for their independence. Ever since the outbreak of the war, a semiclandestine organization called Hortalez & Cie, set up by the wily Parisian playwright whose nommé de plume was Caron de Beaumarchais, had been busy supplying the rebels with munitions and other materials of war. Meanwhile, St. Germain and his war office had been conspiring with Benjamin Franklin, the colonies' unofficial ambassador, and Silas Deane, his special partner for personnel procurement, in recruiting top-drawer soldiers of fortune for high command posts in the shockingly understaffed Colonial Army.

Among the many grave deficiencies in the Colonial Army, the first to be rectified were those of the engineers corps, since engineering was a branch of military science in which France then led the world. Once this lack had been supplied, by such specialists as Du Portail and his confreres, the priority passed to troop training, but here the colonial commissioners in Paris encountered two major obstacles. One was that the British, by now fully aware that France was giving the colonies all aid possible short of war, might well regard the dispatch of a high-ranking French specialist in troop training as a breach of neutrality so flagrant as to constitute a *casus belli*. The other was that, in any case, while French engineers were the world's best, the staff and discipline departments of the French Army were markedly inferior to those of the Prussian.

Of Prussia's superiority in matters of staff and discipline, no one was more thoroughly aware than St. Germain who had served his own apprenticeship under Frederick the Great before qualifying for his ministerial post by reorganizing the Danish Army in which he had held the rank of field marshal. By corollary, no one could have been better equipped than he to appreciate the true quality of Steuben's military background and training as a Prussian staff officer, of which he possessed a firsthand knowledge. Steuben's nationality combined with these qualities to make him as much the answer to the prayers of the French War Office as he was presently to be the answer to Washington's. St. Germain lost no time in making all this clear to Franklin.

Between Steuben's introduction to Franklin and his arrival in Valley Forge there were certain difficulties to overcome. Appalled by the number of officers to whom the commissioners in Paris had guaranteed high rank and pay in the Continental Army, Congress had recently instructed them to make no further such commitments. Hence, while Franklin and Deane were quite ready to take St. Germain's word for Steuben's qualifications, they were unable to give the latter any assurance that these would be adequately recognized when he reached America. The best they could do was to offer him letters of introduction to Congress and the commander in chief which might or might not have the desired effect. Steuben, who wanted a well-paid and steady job, prepared to return to Germany, to take just such a post which he had just been offered by the margrave of Baden. It was at this point that Providence intervened once more, by two strokes which served to dispel the difficulties.

No sooner had Steuben left Paris than his readiness to leave Europe altogether became intensified by the development of rumors, perhaps similar to those that had previously antagonized Frederick the Great, which this time seemed sure to cost him the new appointment at Baden. Meanwhile, a means of making Franklin's offer more inviting was found in an inspiration on the part of Beaumarchais who—as the pseudonymous author of *Figaro*—was even more of a virtuoso in nomenclatural disguises than Steuben himself. This idea, enthusiastically supported by Franklin, was that if Steuben were equipped in Paris not only with resounding letters of introduction but also with the rank, trappings, and dignity equivalent to his capacities rather than his actual military status, Congress would respond by rewarding him with at least comparable standing in the New World.

Since Steuben had actually acquired, along with his title of Freiherr, a resplendent decoration called the Star of Fidelity while serving at Hohenzollern-Hechingen, the social position, which was actually his weak point, seemed unassailable. What needed bolstering were his military credentials which his genuine abilities could be relied upon eventually to justify. Letters to Congress accordingly omitted from Steuben's *curriculum vitae* the entire period of his attachment to the prince of Hohenzollern-Hechingen. They focused instead on his career under Frederick the Great where his rank was reported to have been that of lieutenant-general rather than captain, and omitted to mention that in any case he had lost it a decade and a half before.

Steuben's debarkation at Portsmouth, New Hampshire,

Lieutenant General Baron Friedrich von Steuben.

in the late fall of 1777 and his subsequent journey over-
land, as described for posterity by his seventeen-year-old
secretary-interpreter, Pierre Étienne Duponceau,* made it
clear that the plans concocted by Franklin and Beaumarchais had worked out to perfection. In Boston, where
Steuben picked up a third aide in the person of Pierre
L'Enfant, to whom their commander in chief was to be
posthumously indebted for designing a capital named
after him, he dined with John Hancock and Samuel
Adams. At Reading, Pennsylvania, he was entertained by
the renowned financier, Robert Morris. When he finally
reached York, Steuben flabbergasted Congress by making
a sporting proposition. He offered to serve as a volunteer
without either rank or pay in any capacity that Washington wanted to put him on condition that, if he could
"contribute effectively to the American cause," he should
eventually be granted an income equivalent to the six
hundred guineas a year which he claimed to have sacri-
ficed by leaving Europe. Congress accepted the deal and
Steuben set out for Valley Forge on the nineteenth of
February, having already sent Washington a copy of Benjamin Franklin's eloquent letter of introduction which
read as follows:

The Gentleman who will have the honor of waiting upon
you with this Letter is the Baron Steuben, Lieut. Genl. in
the king of Prussia's Service, whom he attended in all his
campaigns, being his Aid de Camp, quartermaster Genl. etc.
He goes to America with a true Zeal for our Cause and a
View of engaging in it and rendering it all the Service in his

* See Appendix III.

Power. He is recommended to us by two of the best Judges of Military Merit in this Country: Mr. Le Comte de Vergennes and Mr. Le Comte de St. Germain who have long been personally acquainted with him, and interest themselves in promoting his Voyage from a full persuasion that the knowledge and Experience he has acquired by 20 years Study and Practice in the Prussian School may be of great use in our Armies. I Cannot therefore but recommend him warmly to your Excellency, wishing that our Service may be made agreeable to him.

Of his meeting with his new commander four days later, the baron himself provided an appropriate description in a letter to a friend at home:

Upon my arrival at the camp, I was again the object of more honors than I was entitled to. General Washington came several miles to meet me on the road, and accompanied me to my quarters, where I found an officer with twenty-five men as guard of honor. When I declined this, saying that I wished to be considered merely as a volunteer, the general answered me in the politest words, that "The whole army would be gratified to stand sentinels for such volunteers." . . . On the same day my name was given as watchword. The following day the army was mustered, and General Washington accompanied me to review it. To be brief, if Prince Ferdinand of Brunswick, or the greatest field marshal of Europe, had been in my place, he could not have been received with greater marks of honor than I was.

While Steuben's letter to his European friend may well have reflected accurately the climate of his reception, it was, like some of his other writings including his signature, unreliable as to details. Actually, while his name was once used as the camp watchword, this did not occur until almost a month later. As to his entourage, the addition of a guard of honor was perhaps less conspicuous than the subtraction of his Parisian chef.

After looking into the condition of the larder, the latter inquired as to the whereabouts of the kitchen and was shown to an outdoor fireplace which did duty for a stove. In lieu of cooking utensils, the chef found some greasy strings and rusty wires precariously attached to stakes driven into the muddy ground. Understandably horrified, he gave notice to his employer and hastily departed.

While the conditions that confronted the chef were hardly encouraging, those encountered by his master were perhaps even less so. The army at Valley Forge was, to begin with, not a national army at all but merely a collection of detachments from the various colonies. Some of these had been taught smatterings of English, French, or Prussian drill regulations, but no two units knew the same ones. Steuben had therefore to compose a uniform drill manual before he could start to teach the soldiers how to execute it.

In setting about this imposing task, the baron had further hazards to contend with. One of these, since the start of the next campaign might be less than two months away, was the shortage of time. Another was the even more essential element of language. While the baron was fluent in French as well as in his native tongue, his army and spa life on the continent had given him little chance to pick up English of any sort, let alone the colonial vernacular. Unlike his chef, however, he did not let such details deter him; and to balance his liabilities he had at least one valuable asset. This was the wholehearted cooperation of the commander in chief who quickly perceived that the new arrival would make an ideal replacement for Conway as inspector general. Washington's views on the matter were diagnosed in a discerning letter from his aide, Colonel John Laurens, to his father, the president of Congress:

"The Baron Steuben has had the fortune to please uncommonly, for a stranger, at first sight. . . . All the genl officers who have seen him are prepossessed in his favor, and conceive highly of his abilities. . . . The General seems to have a very good opinion of him, and thinks he might be usefully employed in the office of inspector general, but I fancy is cautious of recommending it to Congress, as he might appear implacably to pursue a certain person [Conway] to whom Congress gave that post. . . . The Baron's own desire is to have the present rank and pay of Major Genl; not to have any actual command, until he is better known, and shall be better qualified by a knowledge of our language and the genius and manners of the people. Then, if any stroke is to be struck, his ambition prompts him to solicit a command."

In assisting the baron to set about his formidable assignment, John Laurens' role was not confined to filial explanations, since except for Alexander Hamilton he was the only one of Washington's aides who could speak adequate French. With Hamilton, he helped the baron to conduct prompt and diligent inspections of the camp and to convey the impressions gained thereby to Washington in nocturnal conferences at the Hewes house. The outcome of the conferences was a plan whereby Von Steuben would start at once to compose a book of drill regulations which would then be copied and distributed to a special group of fourteen assistants, one from each of the infantry brigades. The assistants would then have each chapter of the new regulations copied into the orderly books for each brigade and regiment, from which additional copies could be handed down to every company and officer. The drilling of the troops, however, was not to be deferred until the drill manual was completed. As soon as the first chapter was ready, the baron would assemble a model company and instruct its members in executing the drill therein described. While they practiced that drill and taught it to other companies, he would be busy writing up the next one.

Among the practical problems presented by the composition of this volume, not the least troublesome was the language barrier. First the baron would write down the commands in his somewhat Germanic French, which Duponceau would translate into literary English. Then Laurens and Hamilton would convert this version into military or colloquial idiom. An even more serious obstacle was that, as soon as the commands were thus finally rendered intelligible to the soldiers, they became unintelligible to their author. This led to confusion soon after the actual inauguration of the baron's system, which was scheduled for Thursday, March 19. On that day, Steuben arose in the dark at three A.M. After a cup of coffee and a pipe, smoked while his valet, Vogel, braided his pigtail, he mounted and rode to the Grand Parade ground.

Among the many mistakes in training routine which Steuben had noticed, the one he wished to correct first was that of assigning the chore of drilling the troops to noncommissioned officers on the ground that it was beneath the dignity of their superiors. By providing in his own person the example of a presumed Prussian lieutenant general who seemed to find it quite appropriate to show privates how to march, turn around, and hold their rifles, he promptly put a new face on this vital matter. Another difficulty had been the complexity of the movements called for in the various European systems employed by the different units. Steuben corrected this by selecting the most essential elements of the Prussian system and drastically simplifying them. He taught the men a medium-speed marching step that worked much better than either the fast or slow steps previously utilized. Among many other reformations, the number of motions in loading and firing was reduced from seventeen to nine. Heretofore colonial troops had been no match for their opponents with bayonets and used them mainly as spits for cooking. Steuben made bayonet practice a major feature of his drills.

The soldiers Steuben was teaching at Valley Forge differed radically from modern draftees being subjected to the acquisition of an obsolete ceremonial. They were battle-hardened veterans who well knew that their chances of surviving the next campaign might well depend largely on how much of his instruction they could absorb. That their eagerness to learn was, moreover, at least equaled by Steuben's to instruct them became clear during one of their first drills when an order to the model troop got confused by its members, of whom some marched in one direction and some in another. Unaware himself of how to correct his command in English, the baron gave a new one which only served to aggravate the mix-up. Losing his temper, he then began to curse in both French and German, causing the soldiers and onlookers to break into chuckles. At this point a young officer from the ranks stepped forward and, addressing the baron in idiomatic French, offered to translate his orders. The baron accepted, the ranks were re-formed, and the maneuver executed properly.

The young officer, Captain Benjamin Walker of the New York Regiment, thereafter regularly assisted the baron on the parade ground. Meanwhile, the baron made a deliberate specialty of his cursing routine, which the men found hilarious. When they committed a major blunder he would berate them first in French, then German, and finally summon Walker on terms which he later recalled:

"Viens, Walker, mon ami, mon bon ami! Sacré! Goddam de gaucheries of dese badauts. Je ne puis plus. I can curse dem no more."

In a letter to his good friend, Baron von der Goltz, the Prussian ambassador in Paris, Steuben gave a characteristically jovial picture of some of his difficulties:

Believe me, dear Baron, that the task I had to perform was not an easy one. My good republicans wanted everything in the English style; our great and good allies everything according to the French *mode*; and when I presented a plate of *sauer kraut* dressed in the Prussian style, they all wanted to throw it out of the window. Nevertheless, by the force of proving by *Goddams* that my cookery was the best, I overcame the prejudices of the former; but the second liked me as little in the forests of America as they did

114

on the plains of Rossbach. Do not, therefore, be astonished if I am not painted in very bright colors in Parisian circles.

If the soldiers at Valley Forge differed in many respects from modern draftees, they also contrasted vividly with their European contemporaries. The baron noted one marked point of difference in a perceptive letter to another friend at home:

"In the first place, the genius of this nation is not in the least to be compared with that of the Prussians, Austrians or French. You say to your soldiers, 'Do this, and he doeth it'; but I am obliged to say, 'This is the reason why you ought to do that: and then he does it.'"

During the next few weeks the baron spent the evenings laboriously writing out instructions which, translated, compiled, and later printed in a volume renowned as "the Blue Book," eventually formed the basis of U.S. Army training until the Civil War. Meanwhile, by day he drilled his model company so effectively that its members were able to transmit their newfound skills to their colleagues with what seemed to Washington to be dazzling rapidity. By adhering to his refusal to accept, let alone to demand, a commission, Steuben endeared himself not only to his commander in chief but also to his brother officers. Their often well-founded suspicion that all European officers were self-seeking adventurers were suspended in his case, and they enjoyed dining at his quarters. Half a century later, Duponceau provided a vivid description of one such occasion:

Once with the Baron's permission, his aids invited a number of young officers to dine at our quarters, on condition that none should be admitted that had on a whole pair of breeches. This was of course understood as *pars pro toto*; but torn clothes were an indispensable requisite for admission, and in this the guests were very sure not to fail. The dinner took place. The guests clubbed their rations, and we dined sumptuously on tough beefsteak and potatoes, with hickory nuts for our dessert. Instead of wine, we had some kind of spirits, with which we made "Salamanders," that is to say, after filling our glasses, we set the liquor on fire and drank it up, flame and all. Such a set of ragged, and, at the same time, merry fellows, were never brought together. The Baron loved to speak of that dinner, and of his *sans culottes*, as he called us. Thus this denomination was first invented in America and applied to the brave officers and soldiers of our revolutionary army.

Within ten days after the training program began, Steuben's success had been recognized by his commander in chief in his General Order for March 28:

The Baron Steuben, a lieutenant general in foreign service, and a gentleman of great military experience having obligingly undertaken the exercise of inspector general in the army, the Commander in Chief, till the pleasure of Congress shall be known, desires he may be respected as such; and hopes that all officers of whatever rank in it, will afford him every aid in their power in the execution of his office. Lieutenant Colonels Davies, Brooks and Barber, and Mr. Ternaut are appointed to act as sub-inspectors; the three former retaining their rank and order in the line.

The Importance of establishing an uniform system of useful maneuvers, and regularity of discipline, must be obvious; the deficiency of our army in those respects must be equally so; but the time we probably shall have to introduce the necessary reformation is short. With the most active exertion, therefore, of officers of every class, it may be possible to effect all the improvement that may be essential to the success of the ensuing campaign. Arguments surely need not be multiplied to kindle the zeal of officers in a matter of such great moment to their own homes, the advancement of the service, and the prosperity of our arms.

According to Steuben's biographer, Brigadier General John McCauley Palmer, "two men, and two men only, can be regarded as indispensable to the achievement of American independence. These two men were Washington and Steuben. . . ." The dramatic appearance of Steuben just in time to turn the Continental Army into an effective fighting force before the opening of the 1778 campaign may therefore have been, next to Washington's own earlier entrance on the scene, the most advantageous providential dispensation of the entire war. However, while his arrival and that of General Gates's letter were the major events that occurred on the day after Washington's birthday, others of comparable consequence followed in short order.

In the opinion of many modern gourmets, the top indigenous seafood delicacy in the U.S. is fresh shad, procurable only in springtime when these energetic fish swim up certain Atlantic coastal rivers to spawn like salmon in fresh water. During the eighteenth century, shad were so much more plentiful, and hence less highly prized, that the roe was customarily thrown away, while the contracts of indentured servants often contained a clause to the effect that they would not be fed shad more than twice a week. Nonetheless, to the hungry soldiers at Valley Forge, shad would have seemed entirely acceptable if they could have acquired some. This seemed most improbable because Delaware River shad rarely swam inland as far as the Schuylkill.

In 1778, the shad not only swam as far as the Schuylkill, but also started to spawn earlier than usual, and thus while the river was still so low that they were unusually easy to catch. When the start of the shad run was observed in late February by the soldiers of General John Sullivan's brigade, who were camped near the river across which they had built a bridge, they spread the word quickly, and plans were soon afoot for taking advantage of this good fortune. Two miles above the confluence of the Schuylkill and Valley Creek was Pawling's Ford, at the junction of Perkiomen Creek with the former. To make sure that the shad reached this shallow spot, a hundred of Light-Horse Harry Lee's cavalry rode into the water, formed a line across the river, and waded their horses upstream while beating the surface with brush switches. Companies of soldiers posted at the shallows then waded in to net the fish by thousands.

The abnormal shad run of 1778 ended the army's winter famine. It provided not only all the fish the camp could eat for the two weeks that it lasted, but also a surplus of several hundred barrels which were salted down for the future. Even the arrival of the shad, however, was only one of a series of blessings which, with the coming of spring, began to shower down on Valley Forge.

The major blessing was, of course, the weather itself, which turned the dark woods green and then brought out the dogwood flowers. The rising thermometer made the scarcity of warm clothes and blankets increasingly endurable. At the same time it encouraged the men to get out of their huts into the sun and the fresh air, with beneficial consequences for their colds, coughs, and itches.

After trying all winter to find a replacement for Mifflin as quartermaster general, Washington had finally prevailed on his best qualified American major general, Nathanael Greene, to take on this thankless assignment. Greene's reluctance to do so was based on the fact that, for him, as for most of his peers, glory was the chief incentive and he was well aware that history rarely conferred laurels upon quartermaster generals. He had acceded to Washington's pleadings only when promised two full-time assistants and the privilege of leading the right wing in the next battle. Within a week of his appointment in mid-March, Greene had made plans for storing two hundred thousand sacks of grain in warehouses accessible to prospective areas of action in the spring campaign.

The roads were improving, the shortage of wagons and wagoners was diminishing, and the new commissary general, Jeremiah Wadsworth, was prepared to make full use of a quartermaster's department which could furnish adequate transport. News came of the arrival of a French ship at Portsmouth with a huge cargo of Hortalez & Cie clothing. On March 11, with the somewhat reluctant assent of Congress, an extra month's pay was issued to the entire camp, to which the commander in chief on his own authority added a gill of rum for each man. Liquor supplies by this time were indeed so plentiful that a list of prices was established for camp suttlers: French brandy, nineteen shillings a quart; West Indies rum, fifteen; Continental rum, ten; gin, nine; and "Cyder Royal," two. Local farmers at last found it worthwhile to establish a market in the camp, for meat, fresh eggs, and vegetables.

St. Patrick's Day was celebrated both at the camp and in Philadelphia, where Irish sentries at the Broad Street jail got so drunk that a group of Continental prisoners, including Major Persifor Frazer, stole the keys and made their way back to Valley Forge. Stacked at the camp by that time were heaps of eight-pound cannonballs brought down from the munitions works at Warwick. The soldiers used them for a game called "Long Bullet" to see who could bowl farthest, and as the spring advanced, other outdoor sports also became popular. "We played at base this evening," reported a private named George Ewing, referring apparently to the derivative of cricket then more commonly called "rounders" and later, with slight modifications, to be known as baseball.

Washington himself, whether or not he ever threw a silver dollar across the Potomac, enjoyed having a catch with his brother officers and sometimes joined a game of "wickets." Allen McLane's band of Oneida Indians amused themselves, and baffled their white comrades, by shooting arrows at a copper coin set up at a range of fifty yards and hitting it with almost every shaft. Surgeon Waldo, writing in his diary, was moved to the point of versification by the spectacle of the camp at play:

> Camp, hills and dales with mirth resound;
> All with clean clothes and powdered hair
> For Sport and duty now appear,

Here squads in martial exercise,
There whole brigades in order rise. . . .
Where all the varying glitters show
Of guns and bayonets polished bright,
One choix at Fives are earnest here,
Another furious at Cricket there.

In late March, word had got out that Howe was about to be superseded as the British commander in chief by his deputy, the newly knighted Sir Henry Clinton—which suggested that the capital might soon be evacuated. Before this clearing of the skies, however, there remained, as of late February, one particularly dark cloud. This was that Major General Thomas Conway, who was still officially the inspector general of the army, though he had not been in camp since his departure in early January, was now involved in a new scheme and this one fully as distasteful to the commander in chief as its forerunners.

7

THAT CONWAY SHOULD have been so persistent in trying to persuade Congress to make him a major general despite the opposition of his colleagues and commander in chief was by no means altogether mystifying. The main reason that Conway—and for that matter, most of his French fellow countrymen—had joined the Continental Army was that, since promotions were hard to come by in peacetime at home, they hoped to improve their status there by their accomplishments in the colonies. Conway had been quite explicit on this point to John Sullivan, a native New Hampshire man of Irish ancestry, who was one of his few admirers at Valley Forge:

"I depend upon my military promotion in rank for to increase my fortune and that of my family. I freely own it to you it was partly with a view of obtaining sooner the rank of Brigadier in the French army that I have joined this."

By gaining his major generalcy in December, Conway had acquired grounds for expecting an equivalent rank in France on his return; and soon after the commander in chief had given him a predictably cold reception at Valley Forge, he had written Congress offering to resign. In York, however, the commander in chief was still under attack by the faction that was hoping to install Gates in his place. Congress accordingly not only refused to accept Conway's resignation but instead appointed him second-in-command of the enterprise that was the first fruit of the strategic thinking of the newly constituted Board of War.

The plan of the Board of War, apparently the brain-child of its president, Horatio Gates, seemed at first glance a fairly reasonable one. Since Burgoyne's defeat at Saratoga had given the colonies almost undisputed possession of the water route to Canada, now frozen and hence traversible on foot, the plan was to make use of it to march to the St. Lawrence River and if possible drive the British out of Canada by taking Montreal. This project seemed the more feasible since there were still numerous French colonists in Canada who could presumably be counted on to collaborate; and the plan might also serve further to enhance the colonial cause at the court of Louis XVI at Versailles.

That what the Board of War described an "an irruption into Canada" also had an additional and quite extraneous political motivation was, however, also obvious from the way in which the scheme had been developed and proposed. Instead of consulting with the commander in chief of the Colonial Army, the Board of War had neglected even to inform him of the project until after Congress had authorized it, on January 22. News of the scheme first reached Washington shortly thereafter in the form of a letter from Gates who, as president of the board, informed him that the project had been authorized, requested a regiment of his troops to help execute it, and enclosed a letter for Major General the Marquis de Lafayette appointing him to command the expedition. The commander in chief was then also requested, as a sort of afterthought, to give the board the benefit of his own views on the expedition.

With his usual self-discipline, Washington urged Lafayette to accept the commission with the words: "I would rather they had selected you for this than any other man." Thereafter, not without a touch of justifiable sarcasm, he replied to the request for his advice on the subject:

> . . . I am much obliged by your polite request of my Opinion and advice on the Expedition to Canada . . . As I neither know the extent of the Objects in view, nor the means to be employed to effect them, It is not in my power to pass any judgement upon the subject. I can only sincerely wish, that success may attend it, both as it may be advancive of the public good and on account of the personal Honor of the Marquis de la Fayette, for whom I have a very particular esteem and regard. Your Letter was delivered him in a little time after it came to my hands, and he proposes to set out for York Town to morrow.

Gates's procedure in sending word of his victory at Saratoga directly to Congress instead of to Washington had been an obvious and intentional rudeness to his superior. His procedure of announcing the plan for an "irruption into Canada" as a *fait accompli* and of putting Lafayette in charge of it, with Conway as his deputy, without asking Washington's approval went considerably further than mere rudeness. To understand the meaning of the latter requires glancing at what lay behind Washington's "very particular esteem and regard" for the young officer in question.

Marie Joseph Paul Yves Roch Gilbert du Motier, Marquis de Lafayette,* was a twenty-year-old sprig of the

* See Appendix IV.

Major General Marie Joseph Paul Yves Roch Gilbert du Motier, Marquis de Lafayette.

French aristocracy who—like his friend, Marie Antoinette —was a living testimonial to the astonishing fact that the enthusiasm for the U.S. revolution which Du Portail had observed in the café society of Paris was, if possible, exceeded by that displayed in and around the court at Versailles. The son of a renowned officer who had died heroically at the Battle of Minden in 1755, Lafayette, when he first heard about the American rebellion in 1776, reacted promptly in a way which he described later in his memoirs: "My heart espoused warmly the cause of liberty and I thought of nothing but of adding also the aid of my banner."

In adding the aid of his banner to the colonial cause, obstacles soon developed which, though markedly different from those that later impeded Baron von Steuben, were perhaps even more formidable. On a visit to England where he encountered most of the leaders of both parties in Parliament and chatted with General Henry Clinton, then home on leave, whom he was to see the next time more than a year later across a battlefield at Monmouth, New Jersey, Lafayette made a splendid impression on everyone, including the historian, Edward Gibbon, who estimated his income at "130,000 Livres a year." However, though monetary considerations in Lafayette's case were the reverse of those that bothered Steuben, even this comfortable competence eventually turned out to be an inconvenience which, on top of several others, nearly proved insuperable.

Recently married to a charming young wife who had just borne him a daughter, Lafayette encountered his first opposition from his own guardian, the Comte de Broglie.

When Broglie finally gave way, he introduced Lafayette to an experienced professional soldier, the fifty-five-year-old Johann Kalb, who with even less justification for the title than Steuben, was known as the Baron de Kalb and who was to keep an eye on him in the wilderness. De Broglie then took Lafayette and De Kalb to Franklin and Deane, who—then still recruiting officers at top speed—agreed to provide both with commissions as major generals. It was at this point in the proceedings that Lafayette's affluence became almost as serious a hindrance in his case as the lack of it had been in Steuben's.

Seemingly assured of good company en route and a suitable welcome on arrival, Lafayette's next move was to purchase a commodious merchant ship, have it outfitted for a transatlantic voyage, and ask eleven other high-spirited friends to accompany De Kalb and himself. Already much talked of at court, the venture drew further attention as it took on the character of a private amphibious task force, and the British ambassador in Paris, the Viscount Stormount, felt, not unnaturally, called upon to remonstrate strongly. The French government—at the moment discouraged about American prospects by Washington's poor showing in the battles of Long Island, White Plains, and Fort Washington—promptly forbade Lafayette's departure, and even Franklin and Deane tried to persuade him at least to postpone it. It was finally only by disguising himself as a postboy that Lafayette was able to escape to Bordeaux where he found De Kalb and the rest of the party who embarked in his yacht, the *Victoire*, on March 26. After one further attempt by the government to stop him in a Spanish port by means of a *lettre de cachet*, the expedition set a course for America on April 20. It landed, on June 13, on an island off the South Carolina coast, whence its leaders rowed ashore and received a gala midnight welcome at the house of a Major Benjamin Huger.

The nine-hundred-mile carriage ride from the Huger house to Philadelphia went off in good style, and the young visitor found himself favorably impressed en route by the "youth and majesty" of the countryside. On arriving in Philadelphia, however, further trouble developed. When they appeared at the State House, expecting a reception appropriate to the hazards they had overcome and the high motives that had inspired them, they were coldly instructed to wait on the sidewalk until someone had time to come out and talk to them. The someone proved to be James Lovell, a delegate from Massachusetts, who was one of the very few who could make himself intelligible in French.

On this occasion, Lovell's limited linguistic powers were not put to a severe test. The sum of what he found it necessary to tell his visitors was brief and unceremonious: "It seems," he said, "that French officers have a great fancy to enter our service without being invited. It is true we were in need of officers last year, but now we have experienced men and plenty of them." The impact of this greeting upon Lafayette and his entourage was summed up later by Colonel Buysson, the hardy officer who was soon to take up residence in the cave at Valley Forge: "It would be impossible for anyone to be more stupefied than we were. . . ."

Stupefied or otherwise, Lafayette responded with characteristic *noblesse oblige*. Instead of recoiling to Paris in a frame of mind that might well have influenced subsequent decisions by his government, he asked only to be allowed to appear before Congress and read the delegates a short note. When permission was granted, he set forth his modest requirements:

"After the sacrifices I have made, I have the right to expect two favors; one is to serve at my own expense,—the other is to serve, at first, as volunteer."

A high-born foreign officer willing to serve without pay and as a volunteer—that is, without a command—was, to say the least, a novelty. Congress now summoned up the good manners to have Lovell and another delegate—who, according to Buysson was "more skillful as well as more polite"—meet with the visitors for another conference in the course of which it was agreed that Lafayette be made a major general. Commissions for the rest of the party were less promptly granted, but De Kalb eventually became a major general also, and the promises made by Deane and Franklin were eventually honored in the case of six of the eleven others.

Washington's first meeting with Lafayette took place at a Philadelphia dinner party soon after the latter's arrival. The young visitor's astonishingly magnanimous reaction to the mean reception accorded him by Congress naturally appealed to the commander in chief as an example of the kind of generous behavior he liked best and encountered least frequently. Between the two a warm friendship promptly developed which resulted in an invitation from Washington to join his staff—or, in the perhaps more appropriate term then current, his "family."

The bond that was so quickly formed between the forty-five-year-old commander in chief and the young French aristocrat had obvious roots. Washington's liking for fatherly figures implied a desire to be as much like them as possible. However, despite his readiness for paternity, he had no children of his own; and though he was fond of his young stepson, Jackie Custis, the latter's character had been only too eloquently outlined by his schoolmaster a few years before:

"I must confess to you I never did in my life know a youth so exceedingly indolent or so surprisingly voluptuous: one would suppose Nature had intended him for some Asiatic Prince."

Even more aptly than Hamilton, Laurens, Tench Tilghman, and the other junior members of his secretarial staff, Lafayette, as a young and brave foreigner in need of advice and assurance, satisfied Washington's need for a son of his own. As for Lafayette, having lost his own heroic soldier-father in infancy and finding himself a stranger in a foreign land, he needed someone to stand in a father's place. His description of Washington and of his feelings toward him leave no doubt that the Virginian general, though he spoke no French and had never been to Europe, filled the role to perfection.

Wounded in the leg at the Battle of Brandywine, Lafayette endeared himself further to Washington on his return to the army by his readiness to share the hardships of the camp and by filial loyalty which set an example to the other foreign officers. On the subject of Conway, for example, though Lafayette considered him "a very brave and very good officer," he had written Washington that Conway had "done all in his power, by cunning manoeuvres, to take off my confidence and affection for you."

The appointment of Lafayette to command the "irruption into Canada" was justifiable enough on the grounds of rank, nationality, and religion, but there were also additional reasons. By making the appointment with no notice whatsoever to Washington, the board's hope was clearly to encourage dissension between the commander in chief and his distinguished subordinate. Subjected thereafter to the constant counsel and influence of a senior French-speaking officer of rank equal to his own as his nominal second-in-command, Lafayette might even eventually join the Gates faction.

In picking Lafayette for such a role, the Board of War had seriously misjudged its man. Alert to the snub already given Washington in the manner of his appointment to the post, Lafayette's prompt reaction was to say that he would accept it only on condition that he remain subject to Washington's orders and report directly to him. He added, according to President Henry Laurens, that "he would not go without a General Officer of the Rank of Major General in whom he could put confidence, and therefore he demanded Genl. McDougal or Baron de Kalb and that their appointment should be through his General"—that is, Washington. By now so well disposed to Lafayette that it was ready to go to any lengths in an enterprise that would eventually damage Washington, Congress not only agreed to these terms but gave Lafayette leave to take six more of his compatriots with him.

Before leaving for Albany, where the expedition was to be assembled, Lafayette stopped off to dine at Gates's house in York. Seated at the right hand of his host, and surrounded by members of the anti-Washington faction, he noticed a startling omission in the postprandial toasts and stood up to rectify this by raising his glass to "The Commander-in-Chief of the Armies of the United States." According to his memoirs, this gesture caused much startled embarrassment. "Some merely raised their glasses to their lips while others put them down untasted."

While the "irruption into Canada" seemed plausible enough on paper, the plan had certain serious practical defects. Among these were that it was being undertaken in the dead of winter, by men who did not know the country, at a time when even the main army at Valley Forge was so short of provisions of every sort that it could barely survive. The best critique of the plan was that provided by Benedict Arnold who had himself led an expedition to Canada two years before. Still recovering in Albany from wounds he had received at Saratoga, he wrote a letter to Gouverneur Morris that touched on these points and added several others. They were that the British garrison of five hundred in St. John's Fort at the foot of Lake Champlain could stand off an army of ten thousand; that even if the Canadians joined the rebels, they would need to be fed and armed; and that even if the rebels reached Montreal, as was unlikely, there were no arrangements provided either for maintaining them there or getting them home again. He ended with a discerning paragraph that went to the heart of the matter:

If it is alledged that the Troops sent on this Expedition, may be replaced by Militia, would it not have been a more prudent Step to have reinforc'd General Washington with them, and enabled him to drive Mr. Howe & his Banditti from the Country, that, once done, Canada falls of course, probably without the Risk or Expence of an Expedition. I am fully persuaded Congress have been precipitated into this Measure by disigning or ignorent men without having the necessary Information on so important an Affair.

On arriving at Albany after a four-hundred-mile horse-back ride over snowy roads, Lafayette soon saw for himself some additional flaws in the project. His instructions indicated that some 2500 troops would be awaiting his arrival but he found only 1200 even potentially fit for duty and "the most part of those very men are naked, even for a summer's campaign." In addition, their pay was in arrears and all were "disgusted and reluctant to the last degree to begin a winter campaign in so cold a country." Gates had assured him that General John Stark would have burned the British fleet on Lake Champlain "before your arrival." In fact, Stark had not even been told "what number of men, from whence, for what time, for what rendezvous I desire him to raise." Even Conway, who was on the spot, had heard from Philip Schuyler and Benjamin Lincoln as well as Arnold "in the most expressive terms that, in our present circumstances, there was no possibility to begin now an enterprise into Canada." At best, the expedition could not be ready to leave in less than five weeks, by which time the melting of the ice on the lakes would make it impractical. Deputy quartermaster, commissary, and clothier generals who were to have provided the necessary supplies were "entirely of the same opinion." Lafayette sat down and wrote sadly to Washington:

133

Why am I so far from you and what business had the board of War to hurry me through the ice and snow without knowing what I should do, neither what they were doing themselves? . . . to run myself through all the blunders of madness or treachery, (God knows what) . . . I have been deceived by the board of War.

To Gates, his tone was one of candid indignation:

We want monney, Sir, and monney will be spoken of by me till I will be enabled to pay our poor soldiers . . . I have seen a letter to Colonel Hay where you tell him that the very same 400,000 dollars you told me were for me, are destinated to him.

Finally he wrote directly to Congress, stating that he had been put in a position which would cause him to be laughed at by good friends in Europe, to whom he had written enthusiastically of the Canadian expedition. By this time, the absurdity of the whole enterprise had begun to be apparent even in York. On March 2, Congress ordered that the "intended irruption be suspended for the present" while praising Lafayette for his "prudence, activity and zeal" and stating that "nothing has or would have been wanting on his part." On March 13, the whole expedition was called off permanently and Washington was authorized to recall Lafayette and De Kalb. Nothing was said about Conway, who presently found himself detailed to stay on in Albany in charge of the post's stores.

The collapse of the proposed invasion of Canada before it had even got started had interesting repercussions. Congress, which had endorsed the project almost unanimously a few weeks before, could now see no good in it whatever. "Except my own, I do not remember three dissenting voices," President Laurens wrote to his friend John Rutledge on March 11, speaking of its previous popularity. "Now,—well, 'I never liked that Canadian expedition' is unanimous." Patently enough the cause of the collapse was spectacular incompetence in both conception and planning, for which the responsibility belonged to the Board of War in general and its president in particular. The Gates boom thus ended as abruptly as it had started five months before. With his fall from favor, the whole move to discredit Washington and replace him sputtered out in a series of angry letters and picturesque pistol fire.

Bereft now of important influence, Conway's first move was a bitter complaint to his former patron, Gates:

> Sir   I was Determined to return to france Last fall, and was Detain'd in my way by Congress. I was sent to Camp Last December to the purpose of Beginning the functions of inspector General. I was prevented by General Washington from fulfilling these necessary functions, and in Consequence I left Camp with a view of pursuing my journey to france. I was Detain'd a second time by congress; the expedition to Canada was propos'd to me; I accepted; repair'd to Albany with the utmost Dispatch, and found Nothing readdy for an Expedition to Canada. I receiv'd orders Last month to remain in command at Albany; this month, I receiv'd orders from president Laurens to repair to Peekskill under the command of General McDougall; now General McDoughall gives me orders to return to Albany, where it will be impossible for me to give any support to either the Western or Northern frontiers, as I have not in albany as

many men as will guard the valuable stores in that place.

This unaccountable way of Boxing me about is not the usage which I ought to expect as a Gentleman, and as an officer. I am the eldest officer you have in your army. I did not sollicit to Come over, I was frequently sollicited by your agent, and I can say that no foreign officer came over upon more liberal and generous terms. . . .

therefore, sir, if you have no occasion for my services I expect Congress will be so equitable as to accept of my resignation, and give me such a Certificate as will justify me in returning to france at the Beginning of a Campaign.

Congress was not of a mind to detain Conway further, and this time accepted his resignation with an alacrity which its author obviously found disconcerting. Writing again to say that Congress had misconstrued his meaning, he asked to be reinstated—a request which, by a vote of twenty-three to four, was tabled without action. In desperation, Conway came down from Albany to argue his case in person. "The door is shut," said President Laurens.

While duels, for obvious reasons, were forbidden to officers on active duty, Conway's sudden restoration to civilian status made him accessible to challenge, and early in July he took the field against Brigadier John Cadwalader. When the latter's bullet smashed through Conway's lower jaw, he remarked with satisfaction: "I've stopped that lying mouth for a while." Apparently on the point of death in consequence of his wound, Conway a few days later wrote Washington a brief and apparently sincere letter of apology:

Sir: I find myself just able to hold the pen during a few minutes, and take this opportunity of expressing my sincere grief for having done, written, or said anything disagreeable to your Excellency. My career will soon be over; therefore justice and truth prompt me to declare my last sentiments. You are in my eyes the great and good man. May you long enjoy the love, veneration, and esteem of these States, whose liberties you have asserted by your virtues. I am with the greatest respect, etc. Thomas Conway.

Perhaps the greatest error in this communication was Conway's prognosis about his own career. He recovered eventually and the following November returned to France where he joined the Colonial Service in which he rose to the position of governor of the French colonies in India. In 1793, after commanding a royalist army in the south of France, he was sent into exile where he died in 1800.

Another duel appeared to be in the making for Wilkinson, whose indiscretion had brought the whole scheme to discredit Washington into the open. Replacing Richard Peters as secretary to the Board of War in January, Wilkinson had dined with Washington at Valley Forge and there seen the letter in which Gates accused him of inventing the quotation from Conway. This led to sharp words between Gates and Wilkinson who then challenged his former commander. On the morning for which the meeting was scheduled, Gates sought out his former aide, put his arm around his shoulder, and, bursting into tears, said that he would as soon shoot his own son. Prepared to take this for an apology, Wilkinson called off the fight for the time being. Later in the year the two men took the field again, but this time both their pistols failed to fire. In 1779, Wilkinson was appointed clothier general, and his army service continued intermittently for the next forty years, including the War of 1812, in which he campaigned as a major general.

As for Washington himself, his own reactions to the machinations that were obviously going on against him at York and elsewhere were characterized by a lofty and almost amused equanimity perhaps best expressed in a letter to his aide, John Fitzgerald, dated February 28:

> I thank you sincerely for the part you acted at York respecting C**y's Letter; and believe with you, that matters have, and will, turn out very different to what that Party expected. G**s has involved himself in his Letters to me, in the most absurd contradictions; M*** has brought himself into a scrape he does not know how to get out of, with a Gentn. of this State and C**, as you know, is sent upon an expedition which all the World knew, and the event has proved, was not practicable. In a word, I have a good deal of reason to believe that the Machinations of this Junto will recoil upon their own heads, and be a means of bringing some matters to light which by getting me out of the way some of them thought to conceal. Remember me in the most affectionate terms to all my old friends and acquaintances in Alexandria and be assured that with unfeigned regard I am, Dr. Sir yr. Affect. friend.

By the end of April, with Conway's resignation accepted and Gates ordered back into the field, any worries the hostile faction might have caused the commander in chief were well in the past, along with the other problems of midwinter. Meanwhile, a piece of good news was about to break which would make all his previous difficulties seem well worth enduring.

8

WHILE WASHINGTON AND his ragged little army were precariously encamped on their snowy hillside beside the Schuylkill River, events elsewhere in the world had by no means been standing still. Especially lively developments had been going forward in the splendid capitals and courts of Europe with which, ever since the outbreak of hostilities, the colonies had been struggling to establish relations by means of what John Adams had so aptly termed "militia diplomatists."

These diplomats—mostly Americans who happened to be traveling or living on the Continent at the time—were under various severe handicaps. First and most onerous was that none of them had more than a smattering of diplomatic usage as developed in Europe over the preceding four centuries. A corollary difficulty was that they lacked official funds and in some cases seemed to expect their expenses to be defrayed by their host countries. A third, even more basic than the first two, was that the crowned heads which then ruled Europe would in most cases have shown little enthusiasm for receiving even affluent and expert missions representing wilderness outposts across the sea which in themselves lacked proper credentials.

The difficulties which the militia diplomats were up against began to be apparent when the senior member of the group—the celebrated Arthur Lee of Virginia, whose brother, Richard Henry, was that colony's representative in Congress—was designated as commissioner to Spain. Lee began by dashing off what amounted to an anthology of mixed metaphors to the Spanish court, explaining that Spain was finally to be enabled to overcome her traditional enemy and last remaining rival in the New World owing to the assistance of an infant Hercules who would help her clip Britain's wings and pinion her forever. He then set forth blithely for Madrid but got only as far as Burgos before being ejected by the authorities, who explained that his eagerness to serve his own country's interests had apparently prevented him from considering the commitments of the government to which he had addressed his suggestions.

No less disheartening than the experience of Arthur Lee was that of his brother William, who, appointed to represent the colonies in Austria, was told that he would be unacceptable as an envoy and subsequently failed to get within a hundred miles of Vienna. Ralph Izard of South Carolina, a "gentleman of fortune" then living in Europe, and assigned to Florence, wisely stayed north of the Alps after the grand duke of Tuscany had coldly advised him that his credentials were inadequate. Most unfortunate of all perhaps was Francis Dana, a prudish Bostonian who, with an ineptitude remarkable even for Congress, was assigned to the court of the profligate Empress Catherine of Russia. Roundly snubbed by all the upper echelons of St. Petersburg society, he applied for advice in his only language, English, to the French ambassador, the Marquis de Verac, who, with the aid of an interpreter, explained the situation to him as tactfully as possible:

"It is very doubtful, Sir, whether the Cabinet of Her Imperial Majesty will consent to recognize the Minister of a Power which has not as yet, in their eyes, a political existence, and expose themselves to the complaints which the Court of London will not fail to make. . . . [Members of the Cabinet] do not understand English. This will render your communication with the Ministers difficult."

After his summary expulsion from Spain, Arthur Lee set off in the opposite direction, for Berlin, where he was informed that he could stay in the city but only as a private citizen and not as a diplomat. Lee's response to this was a letter explaining to Frederick the Great, with as much assurance and as little dexterity as in the one he had dispatched to Madrid, that with America on his side he would have nothing to fear from the British if he allowed colonial privateers to use Prussian harbors and to exchange tobacco on favorable terms for munitions. While awaiting a reply to this optimistic communication, Lee spent much of his time watching the famous Prussian Army at drill, an experience which he felt qualified him to pass along to Washington some advice on marksmanship acquired from a guide who apparently enjoyed practical jokes. When firing their muskets, Lee explained to the commander in chief, Prussian infantrymen always pointed at the ground ten feet in front of them so as "to counteract the elevation which the act of firing gives to the musket."

Possibly because his long correspondence with Voltaire had spoiled him for an exchange of letters with a mentor whose aptitude in this field seemed unlikely to be equally rewarding, Europe's most famous warrior made no response whatever to Lee's admonitions on grand strategy. This failure, however, by no means implied a lack of sympathy with the viewpoint which the would-be envoy had hoped to expound to him. On the contrary, the emperor, for characteristic reasons of his own, was already so much allied with the cause of the colonies that even Lee's clumsiness in letting agents of the British embassy rifle his papers and thus create a local scandal proved insufficiently provoking to alienate his sympathies.

Having successfully bested his major rivals in the Seven Years' War and now, in his sixties, ready for peace and quiet in which to enjoy the fruits of victory as completely as his increasingly uncertain health allowed, Frederick had only one substantial worry. This was what might happen when the old and ailing Elector of Bavaria, who had no children and for whose throne there were several claimants, passed on to his reward. What appeared most likely was that Emperor Joseph II of Austria would then promptly make good his threat to march across the Inn River to take possession of Munich and the surrounding territory. If he did so, Frederick was resolved to stop him, a feat of which, with the best army in Europe at his disposal, he felt eminently capable so long as Joseph was acting alone in the matter. The difficulty was that Joseph II was the favorite brother of Queen Marie Antoinette of France, who was inclined to follow his advice on international affairs if not always on those of a more intimate nature. Emperor Joseph would surely suggest that she persuade Louis XVI of France to come to his assistance. If she succeeded, as seemed likely, the outcome of a Bavarian war would be much less of a sure thing.

Under these circumstances, Frederick the Great's less than impartial attitude toward the American rebellion was understandable enough. Eager that France be preoccupied by hostilities that would prevent her from combining with Austria against him, he spared no effort in urging his ambassador in Paris—Steuben's old friend, Baron von der Goltz—to make clear to the French court what he thought about the war in the colonies. It was, he said, an opportunity for France which she was not likely to enjoy again within the next three generations.

In Frederick the Great's thoughts on the American rebellion, the main error—analogous in a way to that of Arthur Lee—lay in his apparent assumption that the Comte de Vergennes, Louis XVI's foreign minister, needed to have the potential advantages of Britain's embarrassment brought home to him by a German ambassador. In fact, they were the same ones that Caron de Beaumarchais had been expounding since the hostilities had begun; and, as for Vergennes, he had outlined the whole situation in writing long before anyone else of comparable status had even been so bold as to imagine it. As early as 1763, he had predicted that, with the threat of invasion by the French colonies canceled by the Peace of Paris that ended the French and Indian Wars, the American states would feel no further need of the mother country and would therefore, on some pretext or other, proceed to declare their independence. Proved right in this hypothesis, he and Beaumarchais had now risked another prophecy. They pointed out that, as soon as the War of the Rebellion ended, whichever side won would surely feel free to pounce on the French West Indies—unless, what would be even worse, the warring parties should compose their differences and join forces to pounce on the French Indies together. The sole escape from this grim dilemma was for

France to ensure the friendship of the colonies in the postwar era by assisting them to a decisive victory now.

What deterred Louis XVI from accepting and acting upon this undeniably plausible argument was apparently some dim presentiment of what consequences might follow from helping to set such a precedent for successful rebellion of subjects, colonial or otherwise, against a legitimate monarch. This was, of course, the same misgiving that deterred the Spanish court in Madrid which, holding the other half of the New World in far less turbulent subjection, was even more immediately susceptible than France to the consequences of setting such an example. Nonetheless, for Louis XVI and his ministers, the question was very much a moot one, the final answer to which could only be decided by the course of events. The progress of the war in the colonies was accordingly being followed no more intently in York, Pennsylvania, than it was at Versailles, where Marie Antoinette's rash enthusiasm for the colonies had made their cause fully as chic in court circles as it was popular in those of the cafés cited by Du Portail.

In the summer and early fall of 1777, as the war across the Atlantic moved toward its turning point, the center of attention in Paris was the astonishing figure of Benjamin Franklin. By no means in the same category as his militia colleagues, Franklin was not merely an experienced envoy, seasoned by sixteen years as Pennsylvania's "agent" in London where indeed he had attained recognition as a sort of dean of the diplomatic corps composed of his European colleagues. In addition he was a world-renowned savant in an age when savants like the late revered Sir Isaac

Newton, of whom he was considered the peer if not the superior, were accorded a celebrity to be reserved in later times for movie stars, TV clowns and teen-age yowlers. With all this added to the panache of representing a cause so universally applauded in the French capital, it was no wonder that Franklin, from the time of his arrival in 1776, enjoyed there a status surpassing that of any American visitor before or since, with the possible exception of that accorded to Charles Augustus Lindbergh for a few hours after his arrival by air on a May evening almost precisely a century and a half later.

While his colleagues were being snubbed and rejected by peripheral courts all over the rest of the continent, Franklin was welcomed at Versailles, its most inaccessible social and political stronghold. (The great palace offended his Philadelphian sense of decorum no less by the untidiness of its corridors than by the laxity in morals discernible among its habitués.) While Lee and the rest squabbled about their expense accounts and housing allowances, Franklin was not only handsomely entertained by the host government, but also provided with tangible evidence of his popularity in the form of a cozy villa in the fashionable suburb of Passy. It was in this house that Franklin and Beaumarchais directed the shipments of munitions and matériel by Hortalez & Cie—while the court at Versailles was dutifully engaged in such artful diplomatic ceremonies as congratulating the British on their conquest of Rhode Island.

It was here that, soon after his arrival, Franklin had drafted the first proposal for an open alliance between France and the colonies. And it was here too that, on an evening early in December 1777, Beaumarchais came to offer the colonial envoy his congratulations on the victory at Saratoga—and incidentally get his official confirmation of the news. After dinner, Beaumarchais was in such a hurry to convey the juicy details to Versailles that his coachman exceeded the limits of prudent speed, thus causing an accident on the road in which the coach overturned and its occupant suffered a broken arm.

From his bed of pain, as soon as he was allowed pen and paper, Beaumarchais wrote to Vergennes: "This propitious event is balm to my wounds. Some god has whispered in my ear that King Louis will not disappoint the hopes of the faithful friends whom America has acquired for herself in France." To make the moment of crisis even more emphatic, the elector of Bavaria died soon after the New Year, with the result that Joseph II did indeed cross the Austrian frontier. Thereafter developments in Europe followed one another with such bewildering rapidity that a comparatively restrained note was struck by Frederick the Great when he wrote in his own hand to Von der Goltz: "This is the moment for exerting yourself to the summit of your strength. You must force the deaf to hear and the blind to see; and be sure that you wake up the lethargic to some purpose."

The upshot of all the commotion was later to be summed up best by Sir George Otto Trevelyan in his concluding remarks on the period:

"The French Government did not need pressing. A hint was conveyed to Doctor Franklin and his colleagues, that it would be agreeable to His Majesty if they renewed the offer which they had made him a twelvemonth back;

and they acted on the intimation given. Some time was consumed in arranging the preliminaries; it was necessary that Spain should be consulted, or at all events kept informed, at each successive stage of the negotiation; but on the sixth of February 1778 the signatures were affixed to . . . a Treaty of Amity and Alliance, between France and the United States. The French Government . . . solemnly disclaimed all intention to reconquer Canada. No condition whatever was exacted from America, except a promise that she would never purchase peace with Great Britain by consenting to resume her subjection to the British Crown."

Copies of the Treaty of Alliance with France were brought to York for Congressional signature by Simeon Deane, Silas Dean's brother, who sailed on March 8 in the fast French frigate, *La Sensible*, which docked at Falmouth, Massachusetts, on April 13. News of the alliance reached Washington in a letter from Deane on the afternoon of the thirtieth, and his reaction was set forth with eloquent brevity in a letter to Congress the next morning: "I believe no event was ever received with more heartfelt joy."

Far too cautious to let himself dwell on the rumored possibilities of a French alliance in the preceding months, the commander in chief knew far better than anyone else what the news signified. In a single stroke it transformed the position of the colonies from that of underdog in the fight to almost sure winner. What had started as a helter-skelter rebellion of thirteen ill-assorted overseas settlements against their legitimate master had now suddenly become a world war in which the united colonies had found an ally in the second most powerful nation in the world. With French sea power to engage the British fleet and bring the colonies not only fresh troops, but also all the armaments and supplies they needed, the result of the war, theretofore doubtful at best, should be assured. There would be serious fighting in the months or years to come, but there need no longer be any serious doubt as to the final outcome.

The commander in chief's sudden exuberance was expressed for all the camp to see on the afternoon of May fourth when he lightheartedly joined a group of privates for a game of wickets. The next day, he issued a proclamation calling for an expression of joy by the whole camp in the appropriate form of a Grand Review.

At nine o'clock on the morning of the sixth, the various brigades would assemble on the parade ground to hear the news of the treaty and discourses on its significance by their chaplains. The latter were to be terminated by a cannon shot after the time limit of half an hour. An inspection of the regiments and their arms and a formation on the parade ground would follow in which, as a special honor to their nationality, Lafayette would command the left of the first line and De Kalb the right of the second. This was to be succeeded by a salute of thirteen guns and then a *feu de joie*.

The *feu de joie*—a ceremony to be simulated on festive occasions for future generations by firecrackers tied in strings so as to explode in rapid succession—was a conventional but difficult exercise. As formally executed by troops lined up in double ranks on the parade ground, it

148

consisted of a running fire of blank cartridges starting at the extreme right of the front rank and proceeding until it reached the end of the line, when it passed to the extreme left of the rank behind. The army had tried a *feu de joie* once before, on the dreary Thanksgiving Day appointed to celebrate the victory at Saratoga. On that occasion the feat had been unsteadily performed, but now, after two months of drill under Steuben, the maneuver went off to perfection.

After the *feu de joie*, the troops raised a cheer: "Long live the King of France." The huzzah was followed by a second salute, a second *feu de joie*, and a second cheer: "And long live the friendly European powers." Then, after the same preliminaries once more, came a cheer: "To the American States." The soldiers, each wearing a festive sprig of green in his cap, marched off the field and were issued a gill of rum apiece as a reward for their exertions.

Washington, his "family," and a few carefully chosen guests watched the proceedings from a specially constructed arbor opposite the center of the parade ground. When they ended, the commissioned officers linked arms in lines of thirteen and marched to a tent where they enjoyed a "profusion of fat meat, strong wine and other liquors," at which wives of several generals and a few local ladies were also present. This collation seemed an appropriate moment for the commander in chief to announce a further item of good news that had reached him just after the Grand Review. Late in April he had written Congress to request that Baron von Steuben be made a major general and officially awarded the post of inspector general. Just after the Grand Review he had received

George Washington, painted by Charles Willson Peale at Valley Forge during the winter of 1777–1778. It shows the general in full uniform as commander in chief of the Continental Army.

word by courier that Congress had acceded to his request on May 2, and just before the banquet, he introduced the baron to his guests as "Major General Baron de Steuben, Inspector General of the Army of the United States." The next morning a general order contained further congratulations:

> The Commander-in-Chief takes particular pleasure in acquainting the army that their conduct yesterday afforded him the highest satisfaction. The exactness and order with which their movements were performed is a pleasing evidence of the progress they are making in Military Improvement & an earnest of the pleasing perfection to which they will shortly arrive with a continuation of that laudable Zeal & Emulation which so happily prevails.

With the French alliance safely established, the one thing left to fear, in the opinion of the commander in chief, was nationwide or Congressional complacency. If, instead of responding to good fortune by trying harder than ever to deserve it, the colonies relaxed their efforts on the premise that the French would now be compelled to finish off the war on their behalf, the alliance might be merely the prelude to disaster. In fact, it very nearly proved to be precisely that within the next fortnight, due not to the overconfidence of the public or of Congress but to a display by Washington himself of rashness as extravagant as it was unusual. What made the display especially ironic was that it not only imperiled his entire army and the Continental cause, but did so at the risk of irreparable ruin to the reputation of the very person for whose benefit it had been undertaken, namely the commander in chief's particular protégé, the Marquis de Lafayette.

Even before May, rumors had reached headquarters at Valley Forge that the British were planning to evacuate Philadelphia and move to the north. News of the French alliance made the rumors seem likely enough, since the British might well have heard it first, and since the arrival of a French fleet—perhaps by now already on its way across the Atlantic—would no doubt engage the full attention of Admiral Lord Howe and thus jeopardize his brother's supply lines. That Washington in any case needed to learn all that he could about the impending British response to the new circumstances was obvious enough. What was surprising was that, instead of acquiring the necessary information from scouting details, prisoners picked off British outposts, and the reports brought in by his own well-developed spy network, he chose a far more elaborate and costly expedient. This was to place twenty-two hundred men—representing roughly a third of the able-bodied troops then available in camp—under Lafayette's command with orders to "march towards the enemy's lines."

Lafayette's mission was defined as that of "being a security to this camp and a cover to the country between the Delaware and the Schuylkill, to obstruct the incursions of the enemy's parties and to obtain intelligence of their motions and designs. This last . . . ought to claim your particular attention." The twenty-year-old major general was further admonished that, since his detachment was "a very valuable one and that any accident happening to it would be a very severe blow to this army," he should use every care "to guard against a surprise."

That Washington was so fully aware of the high stakes involved makes all the more puzzling his selection of such a cumbersome and dangerous way of achieving an end which could so readily have been attained with comparative safety and economy. One reason may have been a fatherly eagerness to compensate Lafayette for his disappointment and chagrin over the collapse of the invasion of Canada. Another corollary one may have been to celebrate the treaty with France by giving his top-ranking French officer command for the first time of a substantial force in the field. In any event, it seems clear that, as later noted by Lafayette's aide, the Chevalier de Pontgibaud, the commander in chief was acting "partly out of friendship and partly from policy." Lafayette's detachment comprised Enoch Poor's New Hampshire Brigade, James Potter's Pennsylvania Militia, and Captain Allen McLane's mobile corps of 150, including 50 Indian scouts. They left Valley Forge on the eighteenth of May, crossed to the east bank of the river, and made camp that night—while Howe and his officers were enjoying the Mischianza—on Barren Hill, a modest eminence about eleven miles northwest of Philadelphia and twelve miles east of Valley Forge.

Lafayette's force, while plenty big enough to comprise a potentially fatal loss to the already gravely diminished Continental Army, was by no means big enough to act as an effective screen for Valley Forge against Howe's twenty-four thousand men in Philadelphia. This rudimentary item of tactical arithmetic was quickly perceived by the British commander in chief; and Howe also discerned from a glance at his maps that Barren Hill was the point of convergence of three major highways, all conveniently accessible to Philadelphia. On the eve of his own departure, Howe was far from insensible to the advantages to be gained by taking with him as a prisoner the most celebrated officer in the Colonial Army with the sole exception of Washington himself. On learning of Lafayette's presence on Barren Hill, he lost no time in deciding to make the best possible advantage of it, feeling so sure of the outcome that he invited friends to dinner on the second night after the Mischianza "to meet the Marquis de LaFayette."

Unlike that of Washington on this occasion, the self-assurance of the British commander seemed reasonably well founded. His plan to capture Lafayette and his entire force called for a three-lane sortie from the capital on the night of May 19, involving most of the troops then at his disposal. One column of five thousand men and fifteen guns under Major General James Grant would start first and take a circuitous route to cut Lafayette off from the river fords between Barren Hill and Valley Forge. General Charles "No Flint" Grey of Paoli renown, with two thousand grenadiers and a troop of dragoons, would take a more direct road and attack Lafayette's left flank. Meanwhile a third force under Sir Henry Clinton and Howe himself would box in the rebels from the south. Outnumbered by at least four to one, there would then be nothing left for Lafayette but ignominious surrender.

What actually happened was that all three forces got to their positions in good order but not before Lafayette had been informed of their approach just in time to take evasive action. What the British had failed to discover was that, instead of being obliged to take the main road where Grant was waiting for him, Lafayette could reach nearby Matson's Ford by a shorter side road which led directly from the hilltop to the riverbank. While the British gathered around him and prepared to spring their trap, Lafayette hustled his troops down this road and got them all across the river before the attacking force had even discovered his departure. The result was that when Clinton's men finally moved up to the abandoned post on the hilltop, they met Grant's column arriving from the other side. Thereafter, there was nothing for the three British columns to do except turn around and trudge back to Philadelphia where, according to Lafayette's exuberant account of the affair in his memoirs, they arrived "much fatigued, and ashamed and . . . laughed at for their ill success."

This reminiscence may well have owed much of its jaunty tone to the lapse of time between the incident itself and the author's description of it. Actually, the youthful major general had had an extremely narrow escape which so alarmed Washington—whose first intimation of the difficulties being encountered by his young protégé was the sound of cannon fire on the morning of the twentieth— that he ordered all the troops at Valley Forge assembled and issued forty rounds of ammunition per man, the usual prelude to a major engagement which an attempt to extricate Lafayette would obviously have entailed. It was only a week later, after learning the details of his protégé's escape, that the commander in chief could write an approving report of his conduct to his friend Gouverneur Morris:

"The Marquis, by depending on the militia to patrol the roads on his left, had very near been caught in a snare, in fact he was in it, but by his *own dexterity* or the enemy's *want of it*, he disengaged himself in a very soldierlike manner, and by an orderly and well conducted retreat got out, losing three men killed and a like number taken *only*. . . . Upon the whole the Marquis came handsomely off and the enemy returned disappointed and disgraced. . . ."

While Lafayette was commended and congratulated on his return to Valley Forge on the twenty-third—after reoccupying Barren Hill and staying there for two days—it was noticeable, nonetheless, that, thereafter, Washington refrained from posting a third of his army for intelligence purposes in an exposed position within a day's march of the enemy. And while Lafayette no doubt deserved praise for composure under difficult conditions, there were perhaps others who contributed as much or even more to the successful outcome of the excursion.

One such, according to Chief Justice John Marshall's later account of the affair, was undoubtedly Captain Allen McLane, "a vigilant partisan of great merit" who "In the course of the night . . . fell in with two British grenadiers. . . ." Having been made prisoners, the grenadiers "informed him of the movement made by Grant and also that a large body of Germans was getting ready to march up the Schuylkill." McLane then conveyed this message to his superior just in time to enable him to make his getaway. Some credit for the outcome should also, of course, go to Steuben, whose influence upon the discipline and maneuverability of the army was demonstrated even more dramatically in action at Barren Hill than it had been on the parade ground at Valley Forge a few days earlier. An even more impressive display of Steuben's influence upon the fighting capacity of the Continental Army was to be provided a short time later on a battlefield of even more significance—at Monmouth, New Jersey.

9

Among the human oddities projected into history by the American Revolution, few have provoked more controversy than Major General Charles Lee of Berkeley County, Virginia. Unrelated to the already considerable clan of American-born Virginia Lees, Charles Lee was the physically unprepossessing and consistently unlucky seventh child of an obscure but well-born British colonel who lived in Chester, England. Having launched his own martial career as a lieutenant in Braddock's army in 1755, he had continued it all over the continent of Europe before, as an outspoken Whig, returning to America in 1773, to pitch in his hand with the cause of the colonies.

With his military talents, Lee combined those of a pamphleteer and polemicist, for which the chaotic political situation in the two years preceding the outbreak of war provided him ample scope. Equipped with a courtesy commission as major general in the Polish Army, conferred on him in Warsaw in 1769 by his friend, King Stanislaus Poniatowski, Lee had become sufficiently well-known to be, along with Artemas Ward and John Hancock, one of three other candidates for commander in chief rejected by Congress before it conferred that title on Washington in 1775.

As Washington's deputy and second-in-command, he had been taken prisoner by a roving detachment of British dragoons late in the autumn of 1776. Lee spent the next year confined in New York, where he shared comfortable quarters with the pack of assorted pet dogs whose company he said he preferred to that of humans. Part of this time Lee passed in sessions of cozy reminiscence with fellow officers whom he had known in London and elsewhere and part in composing a document explaining to his captors that the best way to win the war was to split the colonies by means of a campaign in Delaware, Maryland, and Pennsylvania. This literary curiosity, which came to light only in the mid-nineteenth century, has been a vexing puzzle for historians ever since. Some have considered it evidence of flagrant treason on Lee's part while others regard it as merely a typically eccentric peccadillo. What influence it had upon Howe's actual later moves has never been satisfactorily established.

Negotiations for Lee's exchange, which got under way promptly, were assisted by the fact that on British Army records his rank was that of a mere lieutenant colonel. Nonetheless, they were not completed until a U.S. task force, especially assigned to the mission of capturing a British officer who would be regarded as an acceptable equivalent, pounced on an unfortunate general named Richard Prescott at Newport, Rhode Island, where he was dragged unceremoniously out of a bed that he was sharing at the moment with his mistress. Of Prescott, who had already been captured and exchanged once before, it was thereafter said in British Army circles that he was really less an officer than a medium of currency. In any case, with him in hand, a transfer was finally accomplished and Lee returned to the Continental Army on parole early in April. Handsomely welcomed by Washington, he spent one night at headquarters at Valley Forge where, according to Elias Boudinot, the commissary general for prison-

Major General Charles Lee, Washington's deputy and second-in-command. Engraving by A. H. Ritchie after B. Rushbrooke.

ers, who was a fellow guest, he occupied the room adjoining Martha Washington's in company with a British sergeant's wife whom he had brought with him from Philadelphia and smuggled in through the back door. He then proceeded to York where—like his old friend, Sir William Howe, with whom he had just exchanged friendly farewells in Philadelphia, he was an advocate of reconciliation—he urged the wisdom of an early nego-tiated peace. After six weeks' leave at his Virginia tobacco plantation, Prato Verde—bought at the suggestion of his close friend, Horatio Gates, whose house was nearby— Lee had returned to camp to resume his duties a few days after Lafayette's return from Barren Hill.

By this time, news of Howe's recall had reached Wash-ington, along with that of the arrival of a British Peace Commission headed by the Earl of Carlisle and empow-ered to grant the colonies practically all of their war aims except outright independence. In Washington's view, any reconciliation so late in the game would, in addition to breaking the new treaty with France, at best result in an uneasy truce. In such a truce, moreover, the colonies would be at a serious disadvantage, since, if it failed to work and thus gave them cause to rebel a second time, they could scarcely expect the effort to be taken seriously by potential allies in Europe. Having made his views on these points known to Congress, which in due course con-curred, he addressed himself to his own immediate prob-lem which was how to prepare for the summer's cam-paign. Soon after Howe's departure, there were definite signs that the British under Sir Henry Clinton were plan-ning to evacuate the capital. The questions that remained were where they meant to go and how best to deal with each of the numerous possible alternatives.

According to Lee—who perhaps had reason to think he knew—the British would probably launch a campaign in the south aimed at the occupation of the Delaware coast, where they could continue to be supplied by their fleet. Another school of thought suggested that, with a French fleet under Admiral Comte Jean Baptiste d'Estaing already on its way across the Atlantic to keep Admiral Lord Howe's hands full, they were more likely to fall back on New York. In either case, the basic decision for Washington was whether to risk a full-scale engagement in the field or to continue the defensive maneuvering that had caused him to be so sharply criticized the summer before.

Washington's invariable custom, when confronted by a problem in tactics, was to call a council of war in which all the members of his "family" voiced their opinions frankly. On this occasion, by the time he called the conference on June 17, Clinton's army had already started to cross the Delaware and was obviously headed for New York. Washington accordingly asked the members of his staff to submit in writing their views of the best of four possible courses of action: 1) to attack the British immediately; 2) to march across New Jersey by a parallel route without attacking them at all; 3) to harass them en route without risking a major battle; or 4) to attack them with full force somewhere along the road.

All the possibilities except the first found vociferous support. Wayne and Cadwalader—the former always eager for a fight—proposed an all-out attack on Clinton while he was en route, arguing that, even if Clinton won the battle, his baggage train would prevent him from pursuit, while once in New York he would be relatively unassailable. Lord Stirling opposed it on the ground that "if the affairs of the United States can be maintained in their present situation, the enemy loose their point; if we loose a general battle or suffer our army to be much impaired, the United States are ruined." This view was also supported by Steuben who advised following the British on their left flank but avoiding a general action. Lee, quoting the classic advice of the great Spanish captain, Gonsalvo de Córdoba, to the effect that "a Bridge of Gold should be built for a flying enemy," urged that Washington facilitate rather than impede Clinton's retreat to New York. Unfamiliar with Steuben's accomplishments in the preceding months, he continued to reason from the premise that Continental troops were no match for their enemy in the open field.

Before he had determined which one of these alternatives to follow, Washington learned on June 18 that the last of Clinton's troops were already across the Delaware, headed apparently toward Perth Amboy. At Valley Forge, the troops had been alerted for several days, and now, when Washington gave the order to march, they were on the move within two hours. That afternoon, Lee at the head of Poor's, Varnum's, and Huntington's brigades, and Wayne, with what had been Conway's brigade and his own Pennsylvanians, were the first to leave camp. The main body, composed of Lafayette's, De Kalb's, and Stirling's divisions, followed by Knox's artillery, took the road the next morning. A token force of occupation troops moved into Philadelphia the same afternoon, under com-

mand of Benedict Arnold. Still recovering from his
wounds and morose over his treatment by Congress, that
irascible officer found solace in the company of Peggy
Shippen—whose former admirer, John André, was two
years later to hang for his part in Arnold's conspiracy to
betray West Point.

Leaving Valley Forge six months to the day after they
had stumbled up the snowy road from the Gulph, the
army presented a very different aspect on its departure.
When drums sounded to call the men to their posts, they
formed quickly into columns which marched smoothly
across Sullivan's Bridge and through the so-called Fat-
lands North of the Schuylkill toward Doyle's Tavern and
Coryell's Ferry. Using Steuben's new step—"about half
way betwixt slow and quick"—they carried their guns,
with bayonets fixed and gleaming, at a smart angle across
their shoulders. The fifes and drums played songs for the
men to sing as they marched—such lighthearted tunes as
"There's Nothing Like Grog," the privateersmens' favorite; the "Washington Lyric"; and William Billings' "Chester" with its resounding chorus:

> "Let tyrants shake their iron rods
> And slavery clank her galling chains;
> We fear them not, we trust in God;
> New England's God forever reigns."

At the encampment they had left, the charred stumps,
the abatis, the trenches, and redoubts were soon covered
by summer greenery. In the deserted huts, the ashes grew
damp on the hearths and the field mice crept in to nibble

at crusts and bones on the earth floors. Weeds sprouted at the open doorways; and that fall the rain dripped through the unpatched clapboard roofs.

The Battle of Monmouth Court House (now Freehold), New Jersey, was fought on Sunday, June 28, in a ninety-six degree heat wave. It was there that Charles Lee's strange career reached its final turning point, that Steuben's effect on the army was made clear for all the world to see, and that Washington as a field commander had his finest hour. Less dramatically decisive than Saratoga, Monmouth was nonetheless in its way equally significant. It confirmed the results of the earlier, more spectacular victory and showed that the tide of war and of history had turned, finally and irrevocably, in favor of the colonies. The war was to last for five more years, but these were essentially anticlimactic. After Monmouth, it became increasingly apparent how the struggle must eventually end.

The week after the departure from Valley Forge was one of ferocious heat and rain, during which the Continental Army gradually overtook its adversary, marching along parallel roads a little to the north of those followed by Clinton. Obliged to use Admiral Howe's fleet to evacuate three thousand Tories with their household goods, the latter crawled slowly across the sandy flatland with a baggage train eleven miles long, composed of "food, booty, officers' mistresses and other useless things." Further councils of war—which, according to Alexander

Hamilton, "would have done honor to the most honorable society of midwives, and to them only"—led Washington finally to the conclusion that, since Monmouth was within one day's march of unassailable high ground at Middletown, the battle would have to be fought there or not at all. He decided to attack and, having done so, divided his army into an advance section of some five thousand men which would go forward to start the action while he held the rest in reserve, three miles in the rear, ready to administer the decisive blow. Command of the advance force was offered to his deputy, Lee, in line with customary usage.

Still against a general engagement, on the ground that British soldiers were the world's best and colonials no match for them, Lee at first refused the offer, which Lafayette then eagerly accepted. Later Lee changed his mind and claimed command of the advance force as his right—to which Washington, relying heavily on Lafayette's courtesy and common sense, restored him. Half of Clinton's elite troops were marching at the head of his baggage train, under Knyphausen with the elite of the army under Cornwallis at the rear. The maximum objective, if all went well, was to separate the two and accomplish a second Saratoga but Clinton's position was by no means so precarious as Burgoyne's had been, nor was he appreciably outnumbered. Much would depend on how the situation developed; and it was important not to let it develop into a major action unless the colonials had an unmistakable advantage. The outcome might therefore be determined largely by the discretion, and even more by the will and courage, of the general commanding the forward force. In entrusting this force to Lee, Washington had thus at the outset violated one of the fundamental rules of war as later defined by the renowned Napoleonic authority, Baron Henri Jomini:

> To commit the execution of a purpose to one who disapproves of the plan of it, is to employ but one third of the man; his heart and his head are against you; you have command only of his hands.

Fighting began soon after 5 A.M. on the twenty-eighth, when the head of the British baggage train began to move, in the form of a series of disconnected skirmishes under Wayne, Dickinson, and other subordinate commanders—to whom Lee had issued no orders for concerted action the night before. Preparing to move the main body of troops forward to support the advance detachment, Washington got word from Lee that he had surrounded part of Clinton's rear guard of some fifteen hundred men and had hopes of cutting it off. Cheered by this news, the commander in chief rode toward the front astride a new white charger given him the day before by the governor of New Jersey. On the way, however, he was disconcerted to encounter troops retreating in haste and confusion whose officers reported that all the advanced elements had been ordered to fall back. Still on his way forward, he presently met Lee himself, and there occurred the scene—as legendary as that of his outdoor prayer at Valley Forge—when Washington was supposed to have cursed "like an angel from Heaven." There seems to be no doubt that he was furiously angry.

According to Lee, Washington's first words were: " 'I

desire to know, sir, what is the reason—whence arises this disorder and confusion?' (The manner in which he expressed them was much stronger and more severe than the expressions themselves)."

"Sir? Sir?," Tench Tilghman and others heard Lee stammer, and Washington repeated his question:

"What is this confusion about? And what is the cause of the retreat?"

Taken aback by the commander in chief's obvious anger, Lee tried to answer that the retreat had been caused by disregard of his orders on the part of subordinates and by contradictory intelligence. It was, he said, "contrary to my order and contrary to my wishes." But then he added that the attack itself had also been undertaken against his advice.

"Sir, . . . you ought not to have undertaken it unless you intended to go through with it," was Washington's rejoinder and he rode on forward. Lee followed him, and later they met again on a hilltop closer to the front where they were both exposed to British artillery fire. Lee asked for further orders and Washington left him in charge there while he went back to organize the main body.

During the rest of the afternoon, the commander in chief rode from one exposed position to another, ordering and directing the whole battle, as he learned at firsthand from each of his commanders—Greene on the right wing, Stirling on the left, Wayne at the center—how each one was faring. "I never saw the General to so much advantage," Hamilton wrote later. "His coolness and firmness were admirable. He instantly took measures for checking the enemy's advance, and giving time for the Army, which was very near, to form and make a proper disposition."

Lafayette wrote his description in his memoirs many years later: "His presence stopped the retreat . . . his fine appearance on horseback, his calm courage, roused to animation by the vexations of the morning, gave him the air best calculated to excite enthusiasm." The Frenchman recalled how Washington rode "all along the lines amid the shouts of the soldiers, cheering them by his voice and example and restoring to our standard the fortunes of the fight. I thought then, as now, that never had I beheld so superb a man."

In the course of the afternoon, Washington ordered Lee and his troops to the rear. Later he sent Steuben back to re-form them and bring them forward again to support Stirling's wing, then under heavy artillery and musket fire. Steuben re-formed the battalions and marched them forward in perfect order, until they wheeled into position under fire "with as much precision as on an ordinary parade and with the coolness and intrepidity of veteran troops." Hamilton's comment was that until he had seen their behavior he had "never known or conceived the value of military discipline."

An even more spectacular demonstration of the value of Steuben's teaching was provided by Wayne's troops who, fighting from behind a hedgerow in advance of both flanks, were exposed to a series of furious charges by light infantry, grenadiers, and dragoons. Twice Wayne's men held their fire until the most effective moment and then drove the attackers back with grapeshot and bullets. The third charge, under Lieutenant Colonel Henry Monckton, was formed less than five hundred feet from the hedgerow, and Monckton himself led it forward while Wayne gave the order, "Steady, steady! Wait for the word, then pick out the king birds." Not until the British were within forty yards was the word given. The king bird Monckton fell dead so close to the hedge that Americans—this time working with bayonets, as Steuben had taught them to do—dashed out to seize his body and his battalion's flag.

A fourth attack finally flanked Wayne's position and forced him to fall back, but by now the main line had had time to post itself on high ground behind him too firmly to be dislodged. Artillery fire continued until late afternoon when the British retired to a strong defensive position behind a deep ravine just west of the town. Washington tried to launch one more attack in the dusk of the long summer evening, but the light failed before it could get within striking distance and the engagement ended.

Washington and Lafayette bivouacked together that night, their army cloaks spread on the ground, under an oak tree near the battlefield, talking until late in the evening of the extraordinary behavior of Lee. The next day, an insolent letter from that strange commander demanding an explanation from Washington of his angry words on the morning before led to a sharp reply and eventually to the court-martial which ended Lee's army career in disgrace. Victorious for the first time in a major engagement against British troops in the open field, Washington had hoped to renew the battle the next morning, but Clinton made that impossible. Under cover of darkness, he stole away at midnight, and by morning his army was too far along the eastward road to be overtaken before it reached the haven of Middletown.

While the battle of Monmouth Court House effectively ended the story of Valley Forge, there were a few loose ends left of which one had to do with the victory at Saratoga the year before. After his triumph there, General Gates—fearful that Sir Henry Clinton might still find some way to get up the Hudson River to rescue his compatriots—had been eager to get Burgoyne's signature on some sort of a surrender document as soon as possible. The result was the so-called "Convention of Saratoga," according to the specific terms of which Burgoyne's troops were to be allowed to take ship at Boston and return to England on condition that they never be used to fight against the former colonies again. The "Convention troops," as they came to be known, were marched across New England and given quarters of a sort outside Boston, from which many of the higher ranking officers took passage home ahead of them. Meanwhile Sir William Howe —hampered by the shortage of ships and the difficulty of getting them in and out of Boston's icy harbor in the dead of winter—had tried to prevail upon Congress to let the troops embark at New York.

Congress was understandably opposed to this plan—on the grounds that, restored to British command on American soil, the Convention troops might never leave at all. At the same time other obvious defects in the convention that had apparently escaped Gates began to become evident. One of these was the likelihood—quite permissible under the terms of the agreement—that while the prisoners captured by Gates might abide by the terms of the convention after their return to England, they could be used for garrison duty there or elsewhere, replacing other units which could then be exported to America. Since such replacements might well arrive in time for the spring campaign of 1778, the whole effect of the capture of Burgoyne's army would thus be effectively canceled. Washington urged Congress to insist that the British be obliged to live up to the letter of the convention in every respect, thus delaying the departure of the troops as long as possible.

During the winter of 1778, Burgoyne had found occasion to accuse Gates of breaking "the publick faith" in not providing his officers with better quarters. This gave Congress grounds for drawing the inference that the British general had denounced the treaty as a whole; and when Howe finally got his transports to Boston, they were not allowed inside the harbor. Congress now called on the British government to provide an official ratification of the treaty and, when this was not forthcoming, hit on the further expedient of encouraging the prisoners to desert or escape. By March of 1778, Washington was writing to the president of the Council of Massachusetts that: "It gives me inexpressible concern to have repeated information, from the best authorities, that the Committees of the different towns and districts in your state hire deserters from General Burgoyne's army, and employ them as substitutes, to excuse personal service of the inhabitants. I need not enlarge upon the danger of substituting, as soldiers, men who have given glaring proof of a treacherous disposition, and who are bound to us by no motives of attachment, instead of citizens, in whom the ties of country, kindred and sometimes property, are so many securities for their fidelity."

When the fall of 1778 came round, the troops were still in a camp outside Boston, and Congress now devised a new scheme to save firewood and encourage further desertions and escapes. This was to march the remnants of the encampment south to a stockade near Charlottesville, Virginia, a process that had the additional merit of exposing the Hessian troops—of whom the prisoners by now were in large part composed—to special temptations from their fellow Germans on the way through Pennsylvania. Here the Hessians, who were reluctant to escape in New England where they could not make themselves understood by the inhabitants, would find themselves in a rich country whose hospitable residents spoke only German. They could even, for the sake of convenience, be quartered en route at the old encampment at Valley Forge.

Exactly six months after the evacuation of Valley Forge by Washington and a year to the day after the Colonial Army had marched up the road from the Gulph, the three thousand or so of Burgoyne's men who were still prisoners straggled into the camp at Valley Forge and moved into what Major General Friedrich von Riedesel—still sightseeing with his wife and children—described as "three thousand sheds" which looked "like a badly built town." During their week's stay, German officers were allowed, and even encouraged, to travel to Philadelphia and note its prosperity and high morale. Most of the British officers stayed at camp and, as they inspected its defense, wondered why Howe had not attempted an assault on the gradual slope of its southeast approach.

Any hope that the prisoners would melt away into the local population was soon dispelled. In the Pennsylvania Dutch towns farther north, the Hessians had been welcomed by some of the German colonists—who, however, spoke the dialect of a different area and era which made them almost as unintelligible to the German soldiers as the New Englanders had been. At Valley Forge, however, the local farmers of German extraction who had been exposed to Howe's Hessian marauders the year before were in a much less hospitable mood than the country folk around Boston. Said one embittered housewife: "Starve! You shall be made to suffer. You are of our blood, but you sell yourselves for British gold. You came to fight us, to kill us, and to waste our goods and possessions. Now you are our prisoners; it is our turn to torment you."

The hostility of the local population reached its peak at Christmastime when the convention visitors set up little pine trees they had cut in the remaining woods and decorated them as best they could in honor of the day. Other German prisoners, captives from Knyphausen's force the year before who had been put to work in the iron mines nearby, joined their convention countrymen for a holiday celebration. Far from assisting in the revels, the local Germans sided with their Scotch and Irish neighbors in protesting and opposing them. When the soldiers managed to buy some spirits and borrowed the bass viol from a nearby church to accompany their Christmas songs and dances, the farmers called on American guards to stop the noise and insisted that the prisoner restore the viol.

"Our hopes of being received in a hospitable manner by our countrymen were cruelly deceived," one dispirited German prisoner noted in his diary. "They behaved altogether very mean to us. We were ashamed of being Germans, because we had never met so much meanness in one spot from our countrymen. It really does no credit to the character of these Germans that our countrymen were the only ones who treated us mean and tried at the same time to get something out of us and to cheat us. They were also very rude."

Almost the only one of the visitors who received any semblance of a welcome was three-year-old Caroline von Riedesel who went to a housewife, took her by the hand, and said in halting English: "Good woman, I am very hungry." The housewife gave her an egg which Caroline accepted, saying, "I have two sisters." The housewife gave her two more and finally, inviting their mother into the house, gave her bread and milk and allowed her to make tea while she looked on. "The woman eyed the tea lovingly," the baroness later wrote in her diary, "for the Americans love it very much, but they had resolved to drink it no longer as the famous duty on tea had occasioned the war."

Shortly after Christmas, the Hessians got started again on their long road to Charlottesville—often unguarded, sometimes even unguided, sleeping in barns, haylofts, or the open fields. After their departure, the camp was empty again— this time deserted for good. Farmers began to pillage the crumbling huts for fence rails or firewood. On the lower slopes, stumps were pulled or burned out and the ground plowed and planted to wheat or corn. Farther up the hills, the redoubts and gun emplacements were overgrown by brush and weeds; saplings turned into young trees and the forest regained its hold on the hilltops. By the summer of 1787, the old encampment looked much as it had before the army had moved into it almost ten years earlier.

Washington had been spending that summer of 1787 in Philadelphia, as a delegate to the Constitutional Convention that had assembled there in late May. The war had been ended officially with the Treaty of Paris in 1783, but the disorder into which the colonies had fallen thereafter had shown the clear necessity of a Federal Government; and the delegates soon agreed tentatively to the framing of a Constitution which would provide it. On July 26, the convention adjourned for ten days to permit its "Committee on Details" to get down to the actual drafting of this worrisome document. Washington—who had spent the four intervening years in agreeable retirement at Mount Vernon—took advantage of the break to make a trip to the country with Gouverneur Morris at the house of whose unrelated friend and business associate Robert Morris, he was staying in the capital.

The two men drove out of town along the dusty roads behind Washington's horses harnessed to Morris' phaeton —since Washington's had been sent to a carriage maker to be repainted and relined. They stayed over the night of the thirtieth at the house of Mrs. Jane Moore whose 275-

acre property formed part of the old campgrounds. The next morning, Morris, who was an enthusiastic angler, left the house early to try his luck at Trout Run. It was while he was fishing that Washington rode alone to Valley Forge. He was on his way back to the Moore house when he saw the farmers and crossed the field to speak to them.

In the diary which Washington kept so conscientiously from his early boyhood up to within a few days of his death in 1799, there occurs only one noticeable gap. This was the spectacular—and to historians especially regrettable—one comprising his eight years as commander in chief. For Washington's failure to record the most exciting years of his amazing life there were of course sound reasons. One was the risk that such a record might fall into enemy hands. Another was that the details of his doings and his whereabouts were amply recorded in his daily orders, his correspondence, and the memoirs of his associates. In any event, he resumed his diary immediately after the war and the result of his meeting with Henry Woodman was a characteristic entry which recorded his visit to the scene of the Revolution's darkest and most decisive days. The entry reads as follows:

Tuesday, 31st. Whilst Mr. Morris was fishing, I rid over the whole old cantonement of the American Army of the Winter 1777 and 8, visitted all the works, wch. were in Ruins; and the incampments in woods where the grounds had not been cultivated.

On my return back to Mrs. Moore's observing some farmers at work and entering into Conversation with them, I received the following information with regard to the mode of cultivating Buck Wheat, and the application of the grain, viz. The usual time of sowing, is from the 10th to the 20th of July, on two plowings, and as many *harrowings at least*—the grain to be harrowed in. That it is considered an uncertain Crop, being subject to injury by a hot sun whilst it is in blossom and quickly destroyed by frost, in Autumn, and that 25 bushl. is estimated as an average Crop to the Acre. . . .

APPENDICES

The excerpts from the four eyewitness narratives that follow coincide precisely in neither time nor place. The author of each, however, was at Valley Forge for all or part of the winter of 1777–1778. Their separate accounts may thus give depth and vivacity to a scene with which all were familiar—and within which, from time to time, they must also have crossed each other's line of vision.

I

Private Joseph Plumb Martin was born in Becket, Massachusetts, in 1760, the son of an impecunious Yale graduate who was then the Congregational pastor of that western Massachusetts village. During the period described in the following passage he was serving as a private in the Eighth Connecticut Continental Regiment. His memoir of the war—in which he was an active participant throughout—first appeared in a private printing brought out, and perhaps somewhat edited, by his son, in 1830. It was reissued in 1962 under the title Private Yankee Doodle *by the historian George E. Scheer. During his latter years Joseph Martin lived in Prospect, Maine, where he died in 1850 and where his headstone in the village cemetery bears the simple inscription: "Soldier of the Revolution."*

After I had joined my regiment I was kept constantly, when off other duty, engaged in learning the Baron de Steuben's new Prussian exercise. It was a continual drill.

About this time I was sent off from camp in a detachment

consisting of about three thousand men, with four fieldpieces, under the command of the young General Lafayette. We marched to Barren Hill, about twelve miles from Philadelphia. There are crossroads upon this hill, a branch of which leads to the city. We halted here, placed our guards, sent off our scouting parties, and waited for—I know not what. A company of about a hundred Indians, from some northern tribe, joined us here. There were three or four young Frenchmen with them. The Indians were stout-looking fellows and remarkably neat for that race of mortals, but they were Indians. There was upon the hill, and just where we were lying, an old church built of stone, entirely divested of all its entrails. The Indians were amusing themselves and the soldiers by shooting with their bows, in and about the church. I observed something in a corner of the roof which did not appear to belong to the building, and desired an Indian who was standing near me to shoot an arrow at it. He did so and it proved to be a cluster of bats; I should think there were nearly a bushel of them, all hanging upon one another. The house was immediately alive with them, and it was likewise instantly full of Indians and soldiers. The poor bats fared hard; it was sport for all hands. They killed I know not how many, but there was a great slaughter among them. I never saw so many bats before nor since, nor indeed in my whole life put all together.

The next day I was one of a guard to protect the horses belonging to the detachment. . . . Just at the dawn of day the officers' waiters came, almost breathless, after the horses. Upon inquiring for the cause of the unusual hurry, we were told that the British were advancing upon us in our rear. How they could get there was to us a mystery, but they *were* there. We helped the waiters to catch their horses and immediately returned to the main body of the detachment. We found the troops all under arms and in motion, preparing for an onset.

Those of the troops belonging to our brigade were put into the churchyard, which was enclosed by a wall of stone and lime about breast high, a good defense against musketry but poor against artillery. I began to think I should soon have some better sport than killing bats. But our commander found that the enemy was too strong to be engaged in the position we then occupied. He therefore wisely ordered a retreat from this place to the Schuylkill, where we might choose any position that we pleased, having ragged woody hills in our rear and the river in front.

It was about three miles to the river. The weather was exceeding warm, and I was in the rear platoon of the detachment except two platoons of General Washington's Guards. The quick motion in front kept the rear on a constant trot. Two pieces of artillery were in front and two in the rear. The enemy had nearly surrounded us by the time our retreat commenced, but the road we were in was very favorable for us, it being for the most part and especially the first part of it through small woods and copses. When I was about halfway to the river, I saw the right wing of the enemy through a lawn about half a mile distant, but they were too late. Besides, they made a blunder here. They saw our rear guard with the two fieldpieces in its front, and thinking it the front of the detachment, they closed in to secure their prey, but when they had sprung their net they found that they had not a single bird under it.

We crossed the Schuylkill in good order, very near the spot where I had crossed it four times in the month of October the preceding autumn. As fast as the troops crossed they formed and prepared for action, and waited for them to attack us; but we saw no more of them that time, but before we had reached the river the alarm guns were fired in our camp and the whole army was immediately in motion. The British, fearing that they should be outnumbered in their turn, directly set their faces for Philadelphia and set off in as much or more haste than we had left Barren Hill. They had, during the night, left the city with such silence and secrecy, and by taking what was called the New York road, that they escaped detection by all our parties, and the first knowledge they obtained of the enemy's movements was that he was upon their backs, between them and us on the hill. The Indians, with all their alertness, had like to have "bought the rabbit." They kept coming in all the afternoon, in parties of four or five, whooping and hallooing like wild beasts. After they had got collected they vanished; I never saw any more of them. Our scouting parties all came in safe, but I was afterwards informed by a British deserter that several of the enemy perished by the heat and their exertions to get away from a retreating enemy. . . .

II

Dr. Albigence Waldo, who was born in 1750 at Pomfret, Connecticut, served at Valley Forge as Surgeon of the First Connecticut Infantry Division of the Line, which marched from Peekskill, New York, to join Washington's Army in September 1777. Surgeon Waldo's own health, as suggested by his diary, was none too robust; because of its failings, he was obliged to resign his commission the year after the entries that follow. He died in 1794 and his diary was first published in the Pennsylvania Magazine of History and Biography, *Volume XXL (1897).*

December 21.—[Valley Forge.] Preparations made for hutts. Provisions Scarce. Mr. Ellis went homeward—sent a Letter to my Wife. Heartily wish myself at home, my Skin & eyes are almost spoil'd with continual smoke. A general cry thro' the Camp this Evening among the Soldiers, "No Meat! No Meat!"—the Distant vales Echo'd back the melancholly sound —"No Meat! No Meat!" Immitating the noise of Crows & Owls, also, made a part of the confused Musick.

What have you for your Dinners Boys? "Nothing but Fire Cake & Water, Sir." At night, "Gentlemen the Supper is ready." What is your Supper Lads? "Fire Cake & Water, Sir." Very poor beef has been drawn in our Camp the greater part of this season. A Butcher bringing a Quarter of this kind of Beef into Camp one day who had white Buttons on the knees of his breeches, a Soldier cries out—"There, there Tom is some more of your fat Beef, by my soul I can see the Butcher's breeches buttons through it."

December 22.—Lay excessive Cold & uncomfortable last Night—my eyes are started out from their Orbits like a Rabbit's eyes, occasion'd by a great Cold & Smoke.

What have you got for Breakfast, Lads? "Fire Cake & Water, Sir." The Lord send that our Commissary of Purchases may live [on] Fire Cake & Water, 'till their glutted Gutts are turned to Pasteboard.

Our Division are under Marching Orders this morning. I am ashamed to say it, but I am tempted to steal Fowls if I could find them, or even a whole Hog, for I feel as if I could eat one. But the Impoverish'd Country about us, affords but little matter to employ a Thief, or keep a Clever Fellow in good humour. But why do I talk of hunger & hard usage, when so many in the World have not even fire Cake & Water to eat.

The human mind is always poreing upon the gloomy side of Fortune, and while it inhabits this lump of Clay, will always be in an uneasy and fluctuating State, produced by a thousand Incidents in common Life, which are deemed misfortunes, while the mind is taken off from the nobler pursuit of matters in Futurity. The sufferings of the Body naturally gain the Attention of the Mind, and this Attention is more or less strong, in greater or lesser souls, altho' I believe that Ambition & a high Opinion of Fame, makes many People endure hardships and pains with that fortitude we after times Observe them to do. On the other hand, a despicable opinion of the enjoyments of this Life, by a continued series of Misfortunes, and a long acquaintance with Grief, induces others to bear afflictions with becoming serenity and Calmness.

It is not in the power of Philosophy however, to convince a man he may be happy and Contented if he will, with a *Hungry Belly*. Give me Food, Cloaths, Wife & Children, kind Heaven! and I'll be as contented as my Nature will permit me to be.

This Evening a Party with two field pieces were order'd out. At 12 of the Clock at Night, Providence sent us a little Mutton, with which we immediately had some Broth made, & a fine Stomach for same. Ye who Eat Pumpkin Pie and Roast Turkies, and yet Curse fortune for using you ill, Curse her no more, least she reduce your Allowance of her favours to a bit of Fire Cake, & a draught of Cold Water, & in Cold Weather too.

December 23.—The Party that went out last evening not Return'd to Day. This evening an excellent Player on the Violin in that soft kind of Musick, which is so finely adapted to stirr up the tender Passions, while he was playing in the next Tent to mine, these kind of soft Airs it immediately called up in remembrance all the endearing expressions, the Tender Sentiments, the sympathetic friendship that has given so much satisfaction and sensible pleasure to me from the first time I gained the heart & affections of the tenderest of the Fair. A thousand agreeable little incidents which have Occurr'd since our happy connection, and which would have pass'd totally unnoticed by such who are strangers to the soft & sincere passion of Love, were now recall'd to my mind, and filled me with these tender emotions, and Agreeable Reflections, which cannot be described, and which in spite of my Philosophy forced out the sympathetic tear. I wish'd to have the Musick Cease, and yet dreaded its ceasing, least I should loose sight of these dear Ideas, which gave me pain and pleasure at the same instant. Ah Heaven why is it that our harder fate so often deprives us of the enjoyment of what we most wish to enjoy this side of thy brighter realms. There is something in this strong passion of Love far more agreeable than what we can derive from any of the other Passions and which Duller Souls & Cheerless minds are insensible of, & laugh at—let such fools laugh at me.

December 24.—Party of the 22ᵈ not returned. Hutts go on Slowly—Cold & Smoke make us fret. But mankind are always fretting, even if they have more than their proportion of the Blessings of Life. We are never Easy, allways repining at the Providence of an Allwise & Benevolent Being, Blaming Our Country or Faulting our Friends. But I don't know of anything that vexes a man's Soul more than hot smoke continually blowing into his Eyes, & when he attempts to avoid it, is met by a cold and piercing Wind.

December 25, Christmas.—We are still in Tents—when we ought to be in huts—the poor Sick, suffer much in Tents this cold Weather. But we now treat them differently from what they used to be at home, under the inspection of Old Women and Doct. Bolus Linctus. We give them Mutton & Grogg and a Capital Medicine once in a While, to start the Disease from its foundation at once. We avoid Piddling Pills, Powders, Bolus's Linctus's Cordials and all such insignificant matters whose powers are Only render'd important by causing the Patient to vomit up his money instead of his disease. But very few of the sick Men Die.[1]

December 26.—Party of the 22^d not Return'd. The Enemy have been some Days the west Schuylkill from Opposite the City to Derby. Their intentions not yet known. The City is at present pretty Clear of them. Why don't his Excellency rush in & retake the City, in which he will doubtless find much Plunder? Because he knows better than to leave his Post and be catch'd like a d——d fool cooped up in the City. He has always acted wisely hitherto. His conduct when closely scrutinised is uncensurable. Were his Inferior Generals as skillfull as himself, we should have the grandest Choir of Officers ever God made. Many Country Gentlemen in the interior parts of the States who get wrong information of the Affairs & state of our Camp, are very much Surprized at G^l Washington's delay to drive off the Enemy, being falsely inform'd that his Army consists of double the Number of the Enemy's—such wrong information serves not to keep up the spirit of the People, as they must be by and by undeceiv'd to their no small disappointment;—it brings blame on his Excellency, who is deserving of the greatest encomiums; it brings disgrace on the Continental Troops, who have never evidenced the least backwardness in doing their duty, but on the contrary, have cheerfully endur'd a long and very fatigueing Campaign. 'Tis true they have fought but little this Campaign; which is not owing to any Unwillingness in Officers or Soldiers, but for want of convenient Opportunities, which have not offer'd themselves this Season; tho' this may be contradicted by many; but Impartial Truth in future History will clear up these points, and reflect lasting honour on the Wisdom & prudence of G^{enl} Washington. . . .

---

[1] Two thousand eight hundred and ninety-eight men were reported by the surgeons unfit for duty.

III

*Like those of his contemporary, Private Joseph Martin,
the reminiscences of Pierre Stephen Duponceau were written, more than fifty years after the events described, in 1836
and 1837. They took the form of a series of letters addressed
to a distinguished Philadelphia editor and journalist named
Robert Walsh and later to his granddaughter, Miss Anne L.
Garesché which were published just over a century later in
the* Pennsylvania Magazine of History and Biography, Volume LXIII (1939). *A well-born but far from affluent youth
who, at the age of fifteen, had gone to Paris to seek his fortune, Duponceau had picked up a working knowledge of
English along the way by the time he met Baron von Steuben at the home of the playwright, Caron de Beaumarchais,
and took a job as Von Stuben's private secretary.*

Philadelphia 13th June 1836

My dear Sir.

On our journey to Valley Forge we passed through Lancaster then considered the largest inland town in the United
States. Having arrived there early in the afternoon the Baron
was waited upon by Colonel Gibson and other gentlemen
who invited him and his family to a subscription ball to take
place that evening. The Baron accepted and we accordingly
went. There we saw assembled all the fashion and beauty of
Lancaster and its vicinity. The Baron was delighted to con-
verse with the German girls in his native tongue. There was a
handsome supper, and the company did not separate until two
o'clock the next morning.

From Lancaster we proceeded directly to Valley Forge, where we arrived on the 23rd. of February. On the next day I had the honour of being presented to General Washington and to dine with him that day and the next. He received the Baron with great cordiality, and to me he showed much condescending attention. I cannot describe the impression that the first sight of that great man made upon me. I could not keep my eyes from that imposing countenance, grave yet not severe: affable without familiarity. Its predominant expression was calm dignity through which you could trace the strong feelings of the patriot and discern the father, as well as, the commander of his soldiers. I have never seen a picture that represents him to me as I saw him at Valley Forge, and during the campaigns in which I had the honour to follow him. Perhaps that expression was beyond the skill of the painter, but while I live it will remain impressed on my memory. I had frequent opportunities of seeing him as it was my duty to accompany the Baron when he dined with him, which was sometimes twice or thrice in the same week. We visited him also in the evening when Mrs. Washington was at Head-Quarters. We were in a manner domesticated in the family.

General Washington had three aids; Tench Tilghman, John Laurens, and Alexander Hamilton; Robert Hanson Harrison was his secretary. I soon formed a friendship with Laurens, and Hamilton,[1] as well as with Major Monroe then Aid-de-Camp to Lord Sterling [sic], and since President of the United States. With Harrison and Tilghman I had but a common acquaintance. Laurens was master of several languages. I have a letter from him in Latin, Greek, English, French and Spanish. With Monroe I corresponded almost daily, although our quarters were little distant from each other. After his elevation

---

[1] John Laurens and Alexander Hamilton, both of whom spoke French, were designated by Washington to assist Steuben.

to the Presidency he wrote me a long letter expressive of his remembrance of our former friendship. Had I been ambitious of places here was a fine opportunity afforded me to obtain that end, but I preferred my Independence, and suffered that opportunity to pass unimproved.

The situation of our army during the dismal winter that we spent at Valley Forge has been so oftened [sic] described, and by none in more vivid colours than by Washington himself in his letters written at that time, and which may be seen in M^r. Spark's collection,[2] that I shall forbear to expatiate upon the subject. Suffice it to say that we were in want of provisions, of clothes, of fodder for our horses, in short of every thing. I remember seeing the soldiers popping their heads out of their miserable huts, and calling out in an under tone "No bread, no soldier." Their condition was truly pitiful and their courage and perseverance beyond all praise. . . .

In the midst of all our distress there were some bright sides to the picture which Valley Forge exhibited at that time. M^rs. Washington had the courage to follow her husband in that dismal abode; other ladies also graced the scene. Among them was the lady of General Greene, a handsome, elegant and accomplished woman. Her dwelling was the resort of the foreign officers because she understood and spoke the French language and was well versed in French literature. There were also Lady Stirling, the wife of Major General Lord Stirling, her daughter Lady Kitty Alexander who afterwards married M^r. William Duer of New York, and her companion Miss Nancy Brown then a distinguished belle; there was M^rs. Biddle the wife of Colonel Clement Biddle, who was at the head of the forage department, and some other ladies whose names I do

---

2 *The Writings of George Washington; Being His Correspondence, Addresses, Messages, and other Papers* . . . edited by Jared Sparks (Boston, 1834–1838).

not at present recollect. They often met at each other's quarters and sometimes at General Washington's where the evening was spent in conversation over a dish of tea or coffee. There were no *levees* or formal soirees: no dancing, card-playing or amusements of any kind except singing. Every gentleman or lady who could sing was called upon in turn for a song. As I had a tolerable voice, and some knowledge of music, I found myself of consequence in those *reunions*. I soon learned the favourite English songs, and contributed my share to the pleasures of the company.

Thus the time passed until the beginning of May, when the news of the French alliance burst suddenly upon us. Then the public distress was forgotten amidst the universal joy, I shall never forget that glorious time; I was not yet an American; I was proud of being a Frenchman. Rejoicings took place throughout the army, dinners, toasts, songs, *feux de joie*, and what not. I thought I should be devoured by the caresses which the American officers lavished upon me as one of their new allies. Wherever a French officer appeared he was met with congratulations and with smiles. O that was a delightful time! It bound me for ever to the country of my adoption.

The six weeks that elapsed after the reception of this news, passed amidst the dreams and the hopes of future triumphs. The British evacuated Philadelphia on the 18th of June, and I entered it on the same day.

While we were at Valley Forge Baron Steuben was appointed a Major General and Inspector General of the armies of the United States. To the Post of his secretary, which I then held, he was pleased to add that of his aid-de-camp, which gave me by courtesy the rank of major, which I preserved until I quitted the military service.

I remain very sincerely
your friend and humble servant

IV

Two letters from General Lafayette to his wife touch upon the Conway cabal and the expedition to Barren Hill— in which Private Martin was a minor participant.

Camp, near Valley-Forge,
January 6th, 1778.

WHAT a date, my dearest love, and from what a region I am now writing, in the month of January! It is in a camp, in the centre of woods, fifteen hundred leagues from you, that I find myself enclosed in the midst of winter. It is not very long since we were only separated from the enemy by a small river; we are at present stationed seven leagues from them, and it is on this spot that the American army will pass the whole winter, in small barracks, which are scarcely more cheerful than dungeons. I know not whether it will be agreeable to General Howe to visit our new city, in which case we would endeavour to receive him with all due honour. The bearer of this letter will describe to you the pleasant residence which I choose in preference to the happiness of being with you, with all my friends, in the midst of all possible enjoyments; in truth, my love, do you not believe that powerful reasons are requisite to induce a person to make such a sacrifice? Everything combined to urge me to depart,—honour alone told me to remain; and when you learn in detail the circumstances in which I am placed, those in which the army, my friend, its commander, and the whole American cause were placed, you will not only forgive me, but you will excuse, and I may almost venture to say, applaud me. What a pleasure I shall feel in explaining to you myself all the reasons of my conduct, and, in asking, whilst embracing you, a pardon, which I am very certain I shall then obtain! But do not condemn me before hearing my defence. In addition to the reasons I have given you, there is one other reason which I would not relate to every one, because it might appear like affecting airs of ridiculous importance. My presence is more necessary at this moment to the American cause, than you can possibly conceive; many foreigners, who have been refused employment, or whose ambitious views have been frustrated, have raised up some powerful cabals; they have endeavoured, by every sort of artifice, to make me discontented with this revolution, and with him who is its chief; they have spread as widely as they could, the report that I was quitting the continent. The English have proclaimed also, loudly, the same intention on my side. I cannot in conscience appear to justify the malice of these people. If I were to depart, many Frenchmen who are useful here would follow my example. General Washington would feel very unhappy if I were to speak of quitting him; his confidence in me is greater than I dare acknowledge, on account of my youth. In the place he occupies, he is liable to be surrounded by flatterers or secret enemies; he finds in me a secure friend, in whose bosom he may always confide his most secret thoughts, and who will always speak the truth. Not one day passes without his holding long conversations with me, writing me long letters, and he has the kindness to consult me on the most important matters. A peculiar circumstance is occurring at this moment which renders my presence of some use to him: this is not the time to speak of my departure. I am also at present engaged in an interesting correspondence with the president of Congress. The desire to debase England, to promote the advantage of my own country, and the happiness of humanity, which is strongly interested in the existence of one perfectly free nation, all induces me not to depart at the moment when my absence might prove injurious to the cause I have embraced. The General, also, after a slight success in Jersey, requested me, with the unanimous consent of congress, to accept a division in the army, and to form it according to my own judgment, as well as my feeble resources might permit; I ought not to have replied to such a mark of confidence, by asking what were his commissions for Europe. These are some of the reasons, which I confide to you, with an injunction of secrecy. I will repeat to you many more in person, which I dare not hazard in a letter. This letter will be given you by a good Frenchman, who has come a hundred miles to ask me for my commissions. I wrote to you a few days ago by the celebrated Mr. Adams; he will facilitate your sending me letters. You must have received those I sent you as soon as I heard of your confinement. How very happy that event has rendered me, my dearest love! I delight in speaking of it in all my letters, because I delight in occupying myself with it at every moment of my life! What a pleasure it will give me to embrace my two poor little girls, and make them request their mother to forgive me! You do not believe me so hard hearted, and at the same time so ridiculous, as to suppose that the sex of our new infant can have diminished in any degree my joy at its birth. Our age is not so far advanced, that we may not expect to have another child, without a miracle from Heaven. The next one must absolutely be a boy. However, if it be on account of the name that we are to regret not having a son, I declare that I have formed the project of living long enough to bear it many years myself, before I yield it to any other person. I am indebted to the Marshal de Noailles for the joyful news. I am anxiously expecting a letter from you. I received the other day one from Desplaces, who mentioned having sent a preceding one; but the caprice of the winds, without speaking of English ships, often deranges the order of my correspondence. I was for some days very uneasy about the Viscount de Coigny, who, some of my letters announced, was in a precarious state of health. But that letter from Desplaces, who told me all were well, without mentioning the viscount's name, has quite reassured me. I have also received some other letters which do not speak of his health. When you write, I entreat you to send me many details of all the people whom I love, and even of all my acquaintance. It is very extraordinary that I have not heard of Madame de Fronsac's confinement. Say a thousand tender and respectful things from me to her, as well as to the Countess Auguste. If those ladies do not enter into the reasons which force me to remain here, they must indeed think me a most absurd being, more especially as they have opportunities of seeing clearly what a charming wife I am separated from; but even that may prove to them what powerful motives must guide my conduct. Several general officers have brought their wives to the camp; I envy them—not their wives—but the happiness they enjoy in being able to see them. General Washington has also resolved to send for his wife. As to the English, they have received a reinforcement of three hundred young ladies from New York; and we have captured a vessel filled with chaste officers' wives, who had come to rejoin their husbands: they were in great fear of being kept for the American army. . . .

Camp, near Valley-Forge,
June 16, 1778.

There is no news here; the only topic of conversation is the news from Europe, and to that many idle tales are always prefixed: there has been little action on either side; the only important affair was the one which fell to my share the 20th of last month, and there was not any blood shed even there.

General Washington had entrusted me to conduct a detachment of two thousand four hundred chosen men to the vicinity of Philadelphia. It would be too long to explain to you the cause, but it will suffice to tell you, that, in spite of all my precautions, I could not prevent the hostile army from making a nocturnal march, and I found myself the next morning with part of the army in front, and seven thousand men in my rear. These gentlemen were so obliging as to take measures for sending to New York those who should not be killed; but they were so kind, also, as to permit us to retire quietly, without doing us any injury. We had about six or seven killed or wounded, and they twenty-five or thirty, which did not make them amends for a march, in which one part of the army had been obliged to make forty miles.

Some days afterwards, our situation having altered, I returned to the camp, and no events of importance have occurred since. We are expecting the evacuation of Philadelphia, which must, we fancy, soon take place. I have been told that on the 10th of April they were thinking of negotiating rather than of fighting, and that England was becoming each day more humble. . . .

Lafayette's two letters antedated by almost a half century his triumphal tour of the United States. Circumstances had changed considerably by that time, on both sides of the Atlantic. A contemporary account, "written by persons who were present," describes his activities on Saturday, October 16, 1824:

"The General and suite left Washington, and crossed the Potomac on a wooden bridge nearly a mile long. On the Virginia side, he was welcomed to the 'Ancient Dominion'. . . . The procession moving in the following order: Capt. Andrews's troop of Washington cavalry in front, followed by about 2,000 troops on foot; the Committee of Arrangements in

195

carriages, the marshal and his aids, the carriage in which were General La Fayette and General Walter Jones, General Jones's suite, and a number of officers of the army and navy, and many from the State of Virginia; next, a carriage in which was seated G. W. La Fafayette and G. W. P. Custis; then came a cart bearing the tent of Washington, which was handsomely decorated with evergreens and surmounted with the national banner. The procession was flanked on either side by the civic escort, consisting of more than 100 gentlemen, handsomely mounted, with blue sashes, cockades and badges. . . . On Washington street there was erected a superb arch, where it halted and formed a line. . . ."

And in the "superb arch," the live eagle was awaiting his cue.

SELECTED BIBLIOGRAPHY

Adams, John. *Diary and Autobiography of John Adams.* 4 vols. Edited by L. H. Butterfield. New York: Atheneum, 1964.

Alden, John Richard. *General Charles Lee: Traitor or Patriot?* Baton Rouge: Louisiana State University Press, 1951.

———. *The American Revolution: 1775–1783.* New York: Harper and Brothers, 1954.

Bakeless, John. *Turncoats, Traitors and Heroes.* Philadelphia and New York: J. B. Lippincott, 1959.

Baker, William S. *Early Sketches of George Washington.* Philadelphia, 1894.

Bliven, Bruce, Jr. *Battle for Manhattan.* New York: Henry Holt, 1955.

Callahan, Knox. *Henry Knox, General Washington's General.* New York and Toronto: Rinehart, 1958.

Commager, Henry Steele, and Morris, Richard B., eds. *The Spirit of 'Seventy-Six.* New York: Bobbs-Merrill, 1958.

Diary of the American Revolution 1775–1781, The. Compiled by Frank Moore. Abridged, edited and with an Introduction by John Anthony Scott. New York: Washington Square Press, 1967.

Du Ponceau, Pierre Étienne. "Autobiography." *Pennsylvania Magazine of History and Biography* 63 (1939).

Ewing, George. *The Military Journal of . . . (1754–1824), A Soldier of Valley Forge.* New York, 1928.

Fisk, John. *The American Revolution.* 2 vols. Boston and New York: Houghton Mifflin Co., 1933.

Flexner, James Thomas. *George Washington.* 4 vols. Boston.

Freeman, Douglas Southall. *George Washington: a Biography.* 6 vols. New York: Charles Scribner's Sons, 1948–1954.

Heaton, Ronald E. *Valley Forge Yesterday and Today.* Norristown, Pa.: Ronald E. Heaton, 1956.

Hughes, Rupert. *George Washington.* 3 vols. New York: William Morrow and Co., 1930.

"John Marshall at Valley Forge, Description by an Eye Witness." *North American Review* 26:8.

Ketchum, Richard M. *The Winter Soldiers.* Garden City, N.Y.: Doubleday and Company, Inc., 1973.

Knollenberg, Bernhard. *Washington and the Revolution.* New York, 1940.

———. *John Adams, Knox and Washington.* Worcester, Mass.: American Antiquarian Society, 1947.

Lafayette, Marquis de. *Memoirs, Correspondence and Manuscripts of General Lafayette.* New York: Published by his family, 1837.

Laurens, John. *The Army Correspondence of Colonel John Laurens in the Years 1777–78.* New York, 1867.

Lossing, B. J. *Pictorial Field Book of the Revolution.* 2 vols. New York: Harper Brothers, 1850.

McMichael, James. "Diary of Valley Forge." *Pennsylvania Magazine of History and Biography* 16 (1892): 129–59.

(Martin, Joseph P.) *A Narrative of Some of the Adventures, Dangers and Sufferings of a Revolutionary Soldier.* Hallowell, Maine, 1830.

Martin, Joseph Plumb. *Private Yankee Doodle.* Edited by George F. Scheer. Boston: Little, Brown, 1962.

Moore, Frank. *Diary of the American Revolution.* 2 vols. New York, 1865.

Rush, Benjamin. *Autobiography.* Edited by George W. Corner. (American Philosophical Society, Memoirs, XXV.) Princeton, N.J., 1948.

Scheer, George F., and Rankin, Hugh F. *Rebels and Redcoats.* Cleveland and New York: The World Publishing Co., 1957.

Smith, Page. *John Adams.* 2 vols. Garden City, N.Y.: Doubleday and Company, Inc., 1962.

Stoudt, John Joseph. *Ordeal at Valley Forge.* Philadelphia: University of Pennsylvania Press, 1963.

Tower, Charlemagne. *The Marquis de Lafayette.* 2 vols. Philadelphia, 1895.

Trevelyan, George Otto. *The American Revolution.* 6 vols. London: Longmans, Green and Co., 1905.

Van Doren, Carl. *Secret History of the American Revolution.* New York: The Viking Press, 1941.

Wade, Herbert T., and Lively, Robert A. *This Glorious Cause: The Adventures of Two Company Officers in Washington's Army.* Princeton, N.J.: Princeton University Press, 1958.

Waldo, Albigence. Diary Kept at Valley Forge. *Pennsylvania Magazine of History and Biography* 21 (1897).

Ward, Christopher. *The War of the Revolution.* 2 vols. New York: The Macmillan Co., 1952.

Washington, George. *Writings.* Edited by John C. Fitzpatrick. 39 vols. Washington, D.C.: 1931–1944.

Weedon, George. *Valley Forge Orderly Book.* New York, 1902.

Wildes, Harry Emerson. *Valley Forge.* New York: The Macmillan Co., 1938.

Wilkinson, James. *Memoirs of My Own Times.* 3 vols. Philadelphia, 1816.

Woodman, Henry. *The History of Valley Forge.* 3rd. ed. Oaks, Pa.: J. U. Francis, Sr., 1922.

INDEX

INDEX

ABOUT THE AUTHOR

NOEL F. BUSCH, a former Senior Editor of *Time* and then *Life*, is the author of many books, including widely read biographies of Adlai Stevenson and both Presidents Roosevelt. His work has appeared in major magazines on both sides of the Atlantic. He is a Contributing Editor of *The Reader's Digest*.